CREATE-A-KITE

By The Editors Of Consumer Guide®

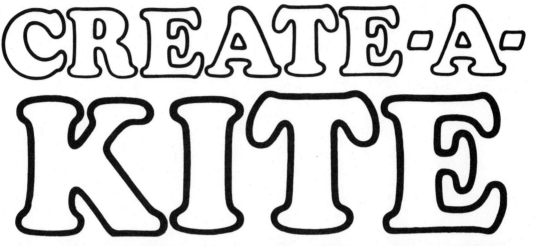

CREATE-A-KITE

How To Build And Fly Your Own Kites

A Fireside Book Published by Simon and Schuster

Contents

Contents

Introduction

FLIGHT, that mysterious, seemingly magical act, has fascinated us since the earliest days of intelligent life on Earth. Primitive people who stalked the land more than 25,000 years ago looked with awe at the birds that soared above them and were so impressed that they went home and recorded the magnificent spectacle on the walls of their caves. Poets, artists, and composers through the ages have heralded the beauty and grace of flight, while ordinary people — intrigued at the possibility of overcoming the force of gravity — have longed to participate in this phenomenon: to create things that fly and then actually guide their creations in flight.

From this overwhelming desire on the part of humanity have come supersonic jets and vehicles capable of traveling to planets in the outskirts of our solar system. But very few people can engage in the creation and guidance of these flying craft. Vast numbers of people, however, can and do participate in creating and flying another form of aircraft — the kite.

Kites are indeed aircraft; they are heavier-than-air objects that must be designed and constructed according to aerodynamic principles, and — like more sophisticated airborne devices — they must be properly launched and controlled in their flight. Kites are, in fact, formally defined as "tethered aircraft." Despite kite-flying's roots in science and technology, though, it is an easy sport to master — one that has been practiced for centuries and one that continues to attract and involve millions of people, from the very young to the elderly, in practically every inhabited area of the globe.

The flying of kites is a sport, an amusement; the creation of kites, however, is an art. This book is devoted to simplifying that art: it is a step-by-step, illustrated manual on how to design, construct, decorate, launch, and fly many different types of kites from the most basic flat and bowed kites to elaborate multi-celled tetrahedral creations.

The Infinite Variety Of Kites

KITES CAN BE as simple or as complex, as individualized, and — within reason — as large or as small as the creator desires; the only limits, besides the aeronautical ones, are the creator's imagination and the materials

Kite-flying is an amusement that attracts all ages.

Kite creation is an art; like airplanes, kites must be designed and constructed according to aerodynamic principles.

available. Kites can be constructed from nothing more than old newspapers and a few strips of bamboo, or they can be colorful, elaborate, hand-painted works of art.

There is an almost infinite variety of kites that the ordinary person can create and fly. Every kite, however, falls in one of the five major types or categories.

- **The Flat Or Plane Kite.** This category includes the common diamond and the square or rectangular, multi-sided, multi-paneled shapes.
- **The Bowed Kite.** Included here are the tailless creations like the Malay Kite.
- **The Delta Kite.** This includes the uniquely designed kites that derive their shape from the Greek triangular-shaped letter.
- **The Cellular Kite.** This category comprises many interesting kites that vary widely in complexity and size, from the basic box kite to many-celled tetrahedral designs.
- **The Flexible Kite.** All the various types of parafoil and sled kites are grouped here.

Within these categories are kites that resemble animals, humans, insects, airplanes, balloons, parachutes, and almost countless geometric designs. Each type of kite, however, has its own individuality of design, its own special requirements of construction, and its own methods of launch and flight. The choice of a kite to create and fly is an individual one, governed only by the creator's preference, energy, and resources.

Kite Lore

TO FULLY enjoy the sport of kite-flying and the art of kite-creating, a person should understand just what a remarkable invention the kite represents. The kite dates back thousands of years. Today, people look on kite-flying primarily as an amusement and sometimes a competition; but over the years kites have served many fascinating, diverse, and important functions.

In the earliest days of kite-flying, more than 2,000 years ago in Asia, the kite was an integral part of religious rituals and festive traditions. Some of these celebrations have even carried over into modern times; the Chinese

Each type of kite has its own special methods of launch and flight.

Festival of Ascending on High is actually a festivity honoring the practice of kite-flying, while the Japanese holiday called Bov's Day (May 5th) — held each year to honor parents who have procreated sons — is highlighted by kite-flying contests and kite battles.

In addition to religion and ceremony, however, kites have also served many utilitarian purposes over the years. Benjamin Franklin's famous experiment in 1752 of flying a kite in a thunderstorm to attract electricity from lightning has unquestionably become the

Although kite-flying is an easy sport to master, fliers are constantly adjusting their kites for top performance.

most famous scientific experiment involving the use of a kite. Even as a child, Franklin knew the kite to be a highly functional device and used one to tow himself in a small boat across a pond. It would be wise to note here, though, that flying a kite in a storm can be very dangerous. Franklin was lucky not to electrocute himself, and no kite flyer should ever fly a kite when there is a possibility of it attracting lightning.

Among other practical applications of kite-flying has been the rather extensive use of kites in the field of meteorology. In the 1800's and early 1900's, kites were used to hoist thermometers, anemometers, and various additional instruments to measure temperature, wind velocity, cloud density, and other weather factors. In fact, as late as the 1930's the United States Weather Bureau maintained a number of "Kite Stations" throughout the country for just these purposes.

Kites have also gone to war. The armies of many nations have used kites to tow torpedoes, lay mines, and serve in a variety of ways as signal devices. In recent times, they have even been used to carry men aloft to observe and scout enemy positions both on land and at sea. As late as World War II, German U-Boats were outfitted with kites for carrying a sailor high above the water to search for enemy ships to attack; in the same war, the United States made widespread use of kites to help tow gunnery targets.

Kites have towed everything from boats to carriages and sleds, raised radio antennas and telephone wires, carried cameras high into the atmosphere for the purpose of aerial photography, and even delivered lifesaving equipment to persons who otherwise might have drowned.

Today, kites take daredevil adventurers soaring in flight in a variety of sports from hang-gliding to water-ski sailing. As a craft capable of carrying man in flight, the kite is in essence an aerodynamic machine that can legitimately be called the precursor of the airplane. In fact, some of the early attempts at inventing the airplane used aerodynamic structures that more closely resembled the kite than modern aircraft. In addition, there have been actual "Kite Planes" based on the elementary principles of box kites and other cellular versions. It is safe to say that the kite's history has not only been a long one but a prestigious one as well.

No one really knows for certain exactly when the illustrious history of the kite began. Chances are it goes back much farther than 200 B.C., the earliest recorded kite-flying. The first kite-flyer is also subject to debate. Some say that a Chinese general named Han Hsin flew a kite over the wall of a fort that he was planning to attack in order to measure the exact distance from his position to the wall. After using the kite to ascertain the distance, Han Hsin then had a tunnel constructed that led inside the fort's walls. Other sources say that the first kite-flyer really was another Chinese military officer, this one named Huan Theng. After realizing that he and his forces were surrounded by the enemy, Huan Theng is said to have created kites outfitted with bizarre noisemakers and sent them flying over the enemy lines, startling his foes into a mad retreat.

Although no one knows exactly when kites were first flown, it is fairly certain that they were invented in China and that they spread from there to Japan, Korea, Indonesia, and the Malay Peninsula. In the 13th century, Marco Polo wrote not only about kite-flying but also about man-carrying kites that he had seen during his travels in the Orient. Earlier, around 700 A.D., kite-flying had spread to the Middle East, and Arabian literature of the time is filled with references to the popularity of the sport. Kite-flying reached Europe in the early Middle Ages, and eventually it made its way to the United States with the migration of people from both Europe and Asia.

All of which brings us to today — the day for which this book is written, the day for us to create our own kites and to take them to the skies.

The only limits to kite creation, besides the aerodynamic ones, are imagination and the materials at hand.

Decorating the Kite

THE FIRST concern in making your own kite is, of course, to put together an aerodynamic creation that will fly easily and well. Decorating the kite, though, is also an important consideration, one that offers a degree of aesthetic satisfaction in the art of kite-creating.

People have been decorating kite covers uniquely and imaginatively for as long as kites have been in existence. Painting kites has even been considered an art form in Japan, but wherever kite decoration is practiced it is a personal expression of the creator's imagination. Done with care, it can be one of the most fascinating and satisfying activities in the creation of a kite.

Planning The Decoration

A KITE COVERING can be decorated in just about any manner provided that no excess weight or bulk is added that might hamper the kite's efficiency in flight. The object is to produce a kite decoration that is not only aesthetically pleasing but also efficient, effective, and incapable of hindering the flight potential of your kite.

In planning the decoration of a kite covering — and planning should always be the first step in the process — consider the structural pattern of the kite. Some kite designs lend themselves to realistic or representational decorations; the bird kite, for example, can resemble as colorful and as exotic a species of bird as the kite-maker can fashion. Kites like the large-surface rectangular kites or the three-stick kites can be painted with traditional faces of Oriental warriors or mythological monsters or any contemporary figure or scene; they can be equally striking and imaginative when painted with abstract designs. Cellular kites, on the other hand, be they box or tetrahedral types, are most often left plain, painted in one solid vibrant color, or decorated with an abstract design.

Principles Of Kite Decoration

WHETHER YOU choose to decorate your kite covering with a representational or with an abstract design, you should keep certain basic aspects of kite decoration in mind. Remember that the airborne kite will be viewed from a substantial distance. Therefore, simple and bold designs are the most effective. The colors you use should also be bold and bright because colors viewed from a distance against a bright sky tend to pale. Vibrant and sharp color combinations can add a great deal to the dramatic effect of the kite, a fact that has been particularly evident in Asiatic kites for many centuries.

If you choose the more realistic or representational type of kite decoration, you can find many examples for scenes, figures, and other decorative elements in illustrations of traditional kites; you can also look for something new to copy from a magazine or book, or you can simply use your own imagination to create the design you desire.

When selecting the paint or coloring material to decorate a kite, keep in mind that you want a paint that dries quickly and that is not too thick. Watercolors or poster paints work quite well, and acrylic paints can also provide handsome, effective coloring. Acrylic paints, however, must be thinned with water because otherwise they tend to crack off when dry. India ink, which comes in various colors, and even food coloring dyes are other good mediums for kite decorations.

Whatever type of paint you choose, be sure to test it first on a scrap piece of kite covering material to make certain that it will create the effect you desire. Different paints and dyes react differently on various materials, and the one you choose may produce an effect or color on the kite covering that is con-siderably different from what you expected.

Once you select the paint and test it on the kite material, take some time to consider the choice of a proper brush for applying it. If the kite cover material is paper, remember that it can be torn quite easily when wet. The brush to use, therefore, is one with soft bristles.

Painting The Kite

THE MOST BASIC and direct method of kite decoration is painting. This method relies solely on the imagination and artistic talent of the kite creator. The finished decoration can be as simple or as elaborate, as realistic or as abstract, as the artist desires.

If you wish to paint a portrait, scene, or design directly on the kite cover, first sketch an outline of it with pencil. Then paint the pencil line in black or another strong, vibrant color. When the outline is dry, fill in the outline with bright paint colors.

Stamping The Kite

YOU ARE NOT restricted to painting as the sole method of kite decoration. There are many other methods from which to choose. One way, for example, involves a printing technique called stamping. You can make a stamp from any of several materials: wood, plastic, styrofoam, linoleum, vinyl, rubber, sponges, even the common potato. Many other household items have inherent shapes which, when stamped on a kite covering, can produce interesting prints — spools, washers, screws, keys, covered cookie cutters, and so forth.

When you have selected your stamp (or stamps), coat it with paint and then apply it to the kite covering. You can apply the stamp in various ways to produce interesting designs. For example, you may wish to repeat a simple stamp design all over the kite; in that case you apply the stamp in straight, even lines across the paper. On the other hand, you may wish to stagger or overlap the stampings. A repeat design or variety of designs that completely print over the kite covering can be very effective.

If you plan to use more than one color, you must allow the first color to dry before adding a second color — unless, of course, you plan to have a color-bleeding effect.

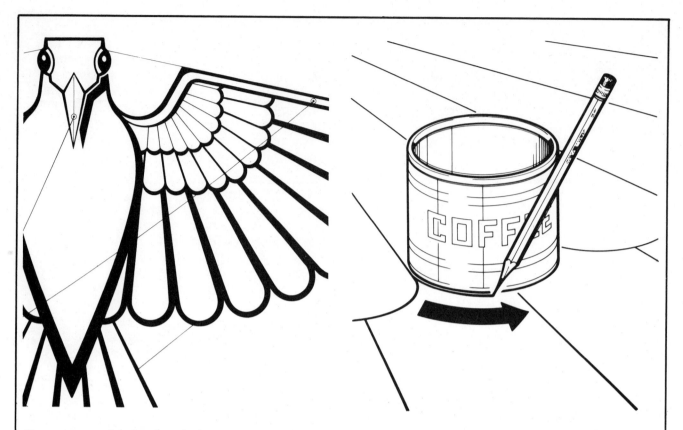

To create curved and scalloped edges, as in the wing sections of the Bird Kite, just use a coffee or other appropriately sized tin can.

All you need is a basic compass to draw the many circles on the face of the Centipede Kite.

A geometric pattern, like the one on the Box Kite, looks complicated, but anyone can draw it with little more than a ruler and a pencil.

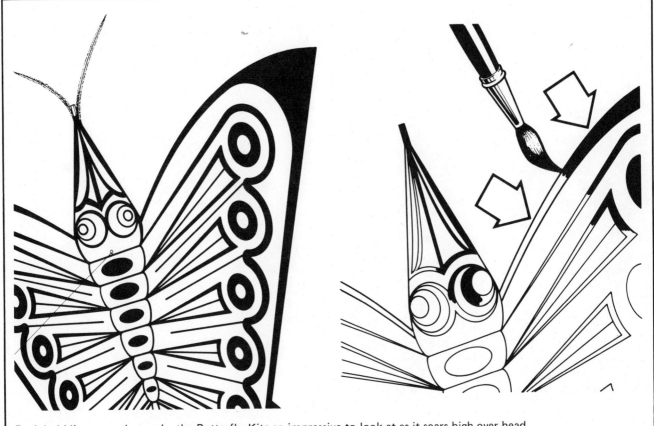

Dark bold lines are what make the Butterfly Kite so impressive to look at as it soars high over head.

The creator's imagination is the only real limit to the myriad ways of decorating the Kite of Circles.

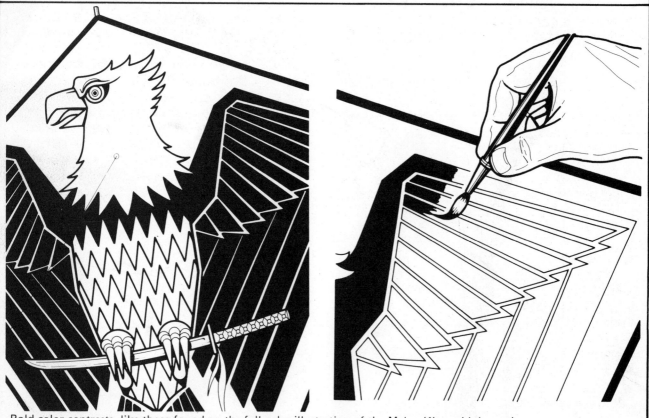

Bold color contrasts, like those found on the full-color illustration of the Malay Kite, add dramatic effect to kite decorations.

Roller Printing The Kite

YOU CAN PRINT, paint or ink colors on the kite cover in different designs by using rollers. Just make sure that you use different rollers for different colors or that the single roller you use is thoroughly clean before applying another color. As with other methods, it is advisable to wait until one color is completely dry before applying a second color, unless you desire a bleeding, blending, or mottled effect.

Patterns can be applied quickly to a kite covering by securing string to a rubber roller with rubber cement in the pattern you wish to reproduce. Then you coat the roller with ink or paint and simply roll the paint-laden roller across the kite covering to print the desired pattern.

Resist-Printing The Kite

ANOTHER METHOD of decorating kite coverings employs what are called resist techniques. Certain materials can be applied to the covering to resist the painting or printing; later, these materials are removed to expose the unpainted or unprinted surface beneath them. For example, strips of masking tape can be applied to the kite cover either in a pattern to produce linear designs or at random to create an abstract effect. When the entire surface of the kite cover is painted, allowed to dry thoroughly, and the strips peeled away, an interesting pattern of the original uncolored surface will be revealed. Spots of other colors can then be dabbed onto the covering to dramatize the linear effect.

Rubber cement can also serve as a resist; it produces a less rigid and more mottled design than the strips of masking tape. After the paint dries, remove the rubber cement by rubbing it with a ball of leftover rubber cement.

Batik The Kite

BATIK IS STILL another form of printing cloth or paper. Similar in principle to resist printing, batik uses melted wax as the resist. The melted wax is brushed on the kite cover in the design to be produced; the areas covered by the wax will remain uncolored when the kite cover is painted. The paint used for batik should be a transparent dye, such as food coloring or India ink.

After applying the melted wax, paint the entire surface of the kite covering with the lightest color dye you plan to use. Wait until the dye is thoroughly dry before proceeding. Then apply more melted wax; the area covered by this wax coating will retain the first color that you applied to the kite cover. Next, paint the complete surface of the covering with another dye color and allow it to dry. You just keep repeating this process until your colorful batik design is finished.

To remove the wax from the kite cover, place the cover between layers of newspaper and then press with a hot iron. The wax will melt onto the newspaper, leaving the colored design on the kite cover. It is, of course, important to remove all the wax which otherwise adds excess weight to the kite.

Dyeing The Kite

YOU CAN DYE both cloth and absorbent paper kite covers. India ink (which comes in various colors), food coloring, and watercolors are all good dyeing mediums.

The simplest way to dye a kite cover is by using the fold method. The first step is to fold the kite cover lengthwise in accordion pleats. If you wish to create a more elaborate design, you can make additional folds. To create an irregular pattern, for example, make unequal folds in the accordion pleats. Keep in mind that the thinner the kite cover material, the more folds you can make and that the more folds you make, the smaller the pattern and the more detailed the overall design will be.

When the kite cover is completely folded, you are ready to dip it in the dye. The area of the folds dipped in the dye determines what colored shapes will be produced. Remember, too, that you can vary the colors by dipping different areas in different dyes. Dip the corners in one color, for example, and then dip the edges in another color. Naturally, the longer the kite cover is left in the dye, the deeper the resulting color will be.

When you finish the dyeing process, carefully unfold the kite cover and leave it to dry. Then, when you are certain that the covering is dry, press the folds or pleats with an iron. If the cover material is paper, be sure to separate it from the warm iron with a covering of rags or newspaper.

Tie dyeing is another common dyeing process. It is, in effect, a fold dye combined with a resist process so that some areas of the cloth (or paper) kite cover are blocked from receiving color. The kite cover material can be folded or gathered together using either rubber bands or strong thread or string coated with wax.

As an elementary form of tie dyeing, you might begin by folding your kite covering in half and then tying it periodically along the length of the fold. Part of this length can then be dipped in one color and another section dipped in a different color. When this part of the tie dyeing process is completed, carefully open the covering and spread it out to dry. Finally, when the covering is thoroughly dry, press it with a warm iron to remove wrinkles.

Miscellaneous Effects

SPATTER PAINTING, like that made famous by the artist Jackson Pollack, is another effective way to decorate a kite — although it is often rather messy. Dip an old toothbrush or stiff-bristle brush of any type in colored ink (India ink works well for this process) and then pull a rigid or bladed object across the bristles to produce a spattering effect on the kite cover. Pieces of paper, rubber cement, tape, or other resist materials can be placed on the covering before spattering to block certain areas and create a specific spattering pattern. When the ink is completely dry, carefully remove the resist material to reveal the original surface.

A marbling effect is another design possibility for paper kite covers. To produce this effect, you float color on top of a viscous or gelatinous preparation called a size. Size can be made by mixing library-type or wallpaper paste with water until you get a thick, smooth substance the consistency of honey. Then strain the size or mix it in a blender to remove any and all lumps.

Next, place the size in a shallow pan. Lay a piece of newspaper on the surface of the size and then strip it off to release any surface tension. Now, place an oil-base paint on the surface of the size and swirl the paint into designs with any pointed object.

When you are satisfied with the design, place your kite covering on top of the paint surface. Be very careful not to trap any air bubbles under the kite cover. Then remove the cover and you will find that the paint design you created in the pan has been transferred to the kite material. Blot away any excess paint and place the kite cover on rags or newspapers to dry. If you wish to make another kite cover design without having to brew up another size, simply remove the old paint from the surface of the size by blotting with newspaper or other absorbent materials.

Kite Attachments

VARIOUS ATTACHMENTS can be added to a kite — some are strictly for decoration, while others serve as noisemakers. Keep in mind, though, that the kite must always be carefully balanced. Therefore, you must add an equal number of attachments to each side of the kite. Any attachment, moreover, should be lightweight; some excellent materials include paper streamers, feathers, tinsel, and dried grass.

Noisemaker attachments can include everything from bells to whistles. Tie whistles securely to a spar with mouthpieces facing the wind, and be sure to maintain the kite's balance. Other noisemakers, such as buzzers and hummers, can also be attached to a kite. A hummer is simply a piece of bamboo that is bowed with a guitar or piano string. It is attached to the back of the kite at the top of the frame where the wind causes it to give off an eerie, moaning sound while the kite is in flight. Buzzers are strips of paper that are fringed along one side and glued securely around a string or spar on the other.

If you want to have a buzzer on your kite (buzzers are especially effective on diamond and star kites), add a second string to the frame just inside the original frame. Attach the covering to the inside string guideline in the normal manner, and then attach buzzers all around the outside frame of the kite.

If you decorate your kite as a face, you may wish to add spinning eyes. The first thing to do is cut two circles out of strong paper. Next, punch two small holes through each circle and insert toothpicks in the holes. Then cut two larger holes in the kite covering where you want the eyes to appear. Finally, tape the ends of the toothpicks to the kite covering so that the eyes are free to spin in the breeze.

These are only a few suggestions to help you decorate your kite. Actually, the number of methods and techniques that can be enlisted to aid in this fascinating process is bound only by your imagination as you go about creating a kite.

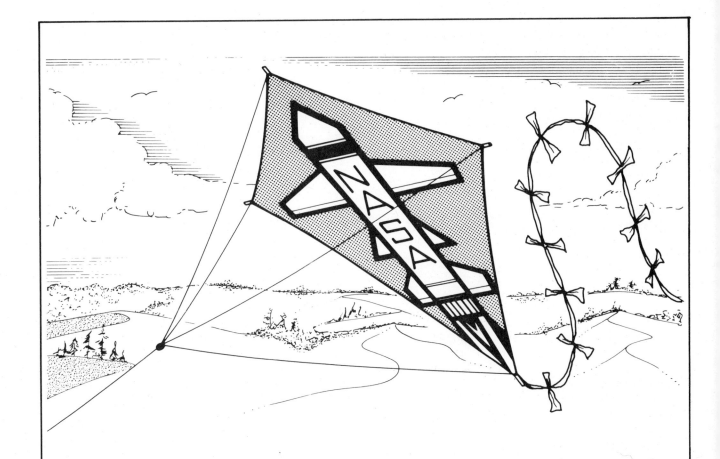

Flying the Kite

BEFORE ATTEMPTING to fly any kite, a person should try to understand the basic aerodynamic principles that enable a heavier-than-air object to stay aloft. Although kites have been flown for several thousand years, it was not until the 19th century that anyone seriously studied how kites fly. The basic principles are really quite simple.

An airplane flies by displacing the air as it moves along. Kites, however, are tethered — that is, they are held in place by the kite-flying line. Air blown against the kite's cover is blocked by the cover and, therefore, forced to move around the kite. If the kite is held at the proper angle to the wind, more air is deflected down around the kite than is forced up and over the kite. This downward deflection of the air flowing around the kite lifts the kite upward, overcoming the force of gravity.

Other factors act on the kite simultane-ously. The flat plane of a kite breaks the wind up into swirls of air turbulence. These turbulence swirls slow the air passing around the kite, reducing the lift caused by the downward deflection of air and increasing the drag. Drag pulls the kite backwards. The kite line, however, prevents the kite from moving backwards, and the net effect of these forces — gravity, lift and drag — is to move the kite upwards.

Getting any kite — from the most basic to the most complex — to fly is a matter of achieving a successful lift-to-drag ratio; that is, the lift must exceed the drag. Naturally, the kite has to be constructed properly and maintained in perfect balance. Assuming that these prerequisites are fulfilled, obtaining the correct lift-to-drag ratio depends on angling the kite to the wind properly, a task which is accomplished by a carefully constructed bridle. Kites with dihedral (two-planed) angles or side surfaces are easier to keep balanced and angled properly. Flat-surface kites, although helped by the curve depressions in their coverings, need tails to react to air turbulence from behind and to provide the necessary stability.

With these aerodynamic principles in mind, consider some of the other conditions necessary for successful kite-flying. The first is the weather. A steady breeze of five to 25 knots is generally considered good kite-flying weather. Different types of kites, however, need different wind conditions to perform at their best. A box kite, for example, flies well on a blustery day, but a small delta kite flown under the same weather conditions would be a dismal failure. The kite, therefore, must be matched to fit the prevailing wind conditions.

The following table makes it easy to judge wind velocity and to select the proper kite to fly. Developed by Admiral Francis Beaufort for determining the speed of wind at sea, these guidelines have since been modified for use on land and particularly for application to kite-flying.

Wind in Knots	Wind Effect	Applicable Kite for Flying
0-1	Calm: smoke rises vertically	None
1-3	Light breeze: direction shown by smoke drift	Very small, lightweight kites only
4-6	Light: leaves rustle; can be felt on face	Small and medium kites (if lightweight)
7-10	Gentle: leaves and twigs put in motion	All kites except very heavy ones
11-15	Moderate: small branches move; wind raises dust	Box kites as well as other medium and heavy kites
16-21	Moderate to strong: small trees sway	Strong and sturdy kites
22-27	Strong: large branches move	Only the very large and strong kites

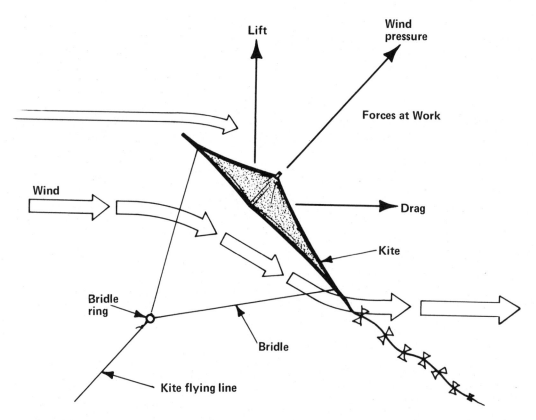

The downward deflection of air flowing around the kite lifts the kite upward, overcoming the forces of drag and gravity.

One final but very important note on the weather: NEVER fly a kite when it is raining or if there is any possibility of lightning.

The next consideration in effective kite-flying is to select the right place to launch the kite and keep it aloft. A large park or open field — a place where there are no trees or buildings to block the wind or to cause air turbulence — is ideal. The beach area near a lake or seashore can also be quite good, although the wind can change direction suddenly. If you must fly your kite in a hilly area, the best position to do it is on the windward side of the hill; the wind, flowing uphill, will aid in lifting the kite. If you must launch the kite in the proximity of buildings or trees, be sure to launch it from a postion as far upwind as possible. Stay far away from other kite-flyers, and never launch a kite near electrical wires, airports, or busy roads.

You Need More Than Wind

TO LAUNCH the kite you have created, you will need more than a conducive wind pattern and an aerodynamically designed kite. Of the additional materials you will need, the most obvious is a line to attach to the bridle or bridle ring. The flying line can be string, nylon cord, or fishing line; fishing line is inexpensive and can be purchased at any sporting goods store in a variety of strengths. Never use metallic wire for a flying line, and never fly a kite with a wet string; both wire and wet string can be dangerous conductors of electricity.

It is an unfortunate but all-too-common occurrence to lose a kite because the flying line breaks. Make certain that the flying line is strong enough to contend with the particular kite and wind conditions in question. Since the flying line also contributes to the kite's drag, however, a line should be chosen that offers as little weight and air resistance as possible. To get a general idea of what a particular kite requires in terms of a flying line, measure the square-foot surface area of the kite (multiply the length by the width by the height). The appropriate flying line should have a break strength three times the kite's square-foot surface area. For example, if the kite has a sur-

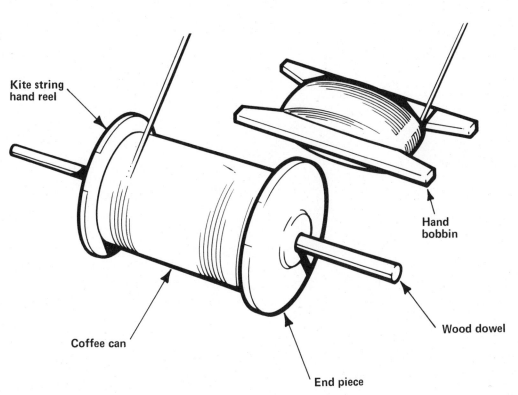

Kite string
hand reel

Hand
bobbin

Coffee can

Wood dowel

End piece

Kite flyers need a reel on which to wind the flying line; you can make a reel out of any large cylindrical object, even a coffee can.

face area of six square feet, the flying line should have a minimum break strength of 18 pounds. A large sled or box kite that is flown in a strong wind may require a flying line with a break strength of as much as 100 pounds. Keep in mind, moreover, that wind conditions can be hard to judge. Even if the wind at ground level is quite manageable, it may be much stronger; it may, in fact, be blowing in an entirely different direction a few thousand feet up.

You will also need a reel on which to wind the flying line. Anything from a simple stick to a fishing reel can do the job. You can even make your own reel out of practically any cylindrical item, even a large hollow can like a coffee can. You will need a strong reel when flying a large kite because it must withstand great tension. Remember, too, that the diameter of the reel determines the number of line revolutions that will be necessary when bringing in the kite; the reel diameter thus determines the amount of time and effort you must expend in retrieving your kite.

It is always wise to wear a pair of gloves when flying a kite — especially large kites.

Gloves can prevent the flying line from cutting your hands.

Plan on having extra tails ready to add to the kite in order to compensate for unexpected wind conditions. In addition, carry a knife and a supply of tape for making repairs and swivel clips for attaching the line to the kite's bridle. The clips not only make it easy to switch the line to a different kite, but they also help prevent the bridle from becoming twisted in the air.

Launching The Kite

BEFORE ATTEMPTING to put your kite in flight, spend some time checking everything thoroughly. First, re-check the kite's balance. When you are satisfied that the kite is well balanced, the next thing to check is the position of the bridle. As a general rule, the bridle should be halfway between the middle and the top of the kite and exactly in the center laterally.

In the case of a flat kite, make sure that you have attached a tail of adequate length. It is probably best to begin with a tail that is four

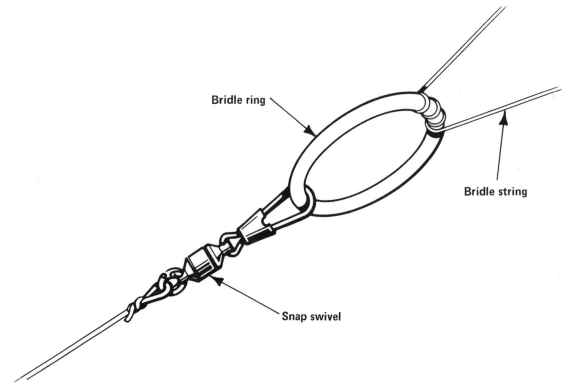

Bridle ring

Bridle string

Snap swivel

A swivel attachment connecting the flying line and the bridle ring is a great help in reducing the frequency of tangled lines.

times the length of the kite's diagonal measurement; then you can adjust this length after a test flight in order to accommodate wind conditions and other flight factors. Hold off on final adjustment of the tail because you may encounter stronger winds at higher altitudes.

Generally speaking, a tail three times the length of the diagonal measurement of the kite is adequate, but the length requirements vary according to climatic conditons. A longer tail is needed on a windy day and a shorter tail on a calm day. In addition, a single tail is usually more effective on a windy day, while a double tail works better on a normal day.

When you finish checking out the kite thoroughly and attaching the flying line securely, the only step left is to fly it. It always helps to have a friend to assist you when you actually get to the point of launching the kite. The friend's job is to hold the kite as you launch it.

First, unroll about 75 feet of line. Then, with your back to the wind, have your helper stand downwind from you and hold the kite vertically as high in the air as possible. The tail should be spread out away from you to help balance the kite as it rises. When the wind is steady, have the helper release the kite and then back up slowly. As the kite rises, gradually release more line, but remember that you must always keep the line taut.

If you do not have a friend to help, you must approach the problem in a slightly different manner. Stand with your back to the wind and hold the kite at its lower edge. Make sure that you hold the kite in a vertical position as high in the air as you can. If you are launching a small or average-size kite, wait until the wind is steady and then gently toss the kite upwards while simultaneously stepping backwards quickly. As the kite starts to rise, gradually let out more flying line. Be sure, though, to keep the flying line taut. If the wind conditons are right, your kite should rise smoothly.

A large box kite (or other cellular or complex kite) may be too difficult to hold for the launch. In such a case, stand the kite on end and gently pull the line toward you, slightly tipping the kite as you do. The wind should lift the kite gently. If the wind is not sufficient to lift the kite, however, you may have to use a winching process.

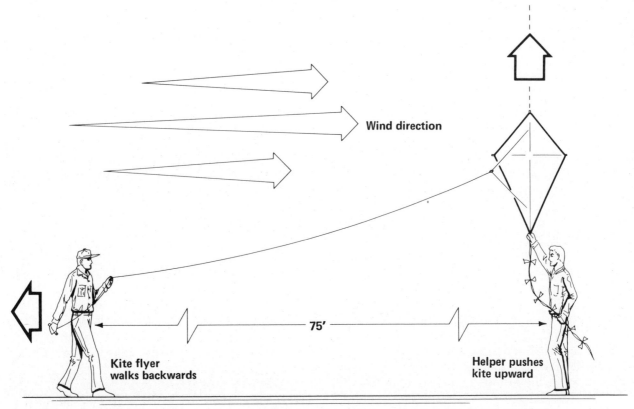

Wind direction

75'

Kite flyer walks backwards

Helper pushes kite upward

In launching the kite, stand with your back to the wind while your helper stands downwind and holds the kite as high as possible.

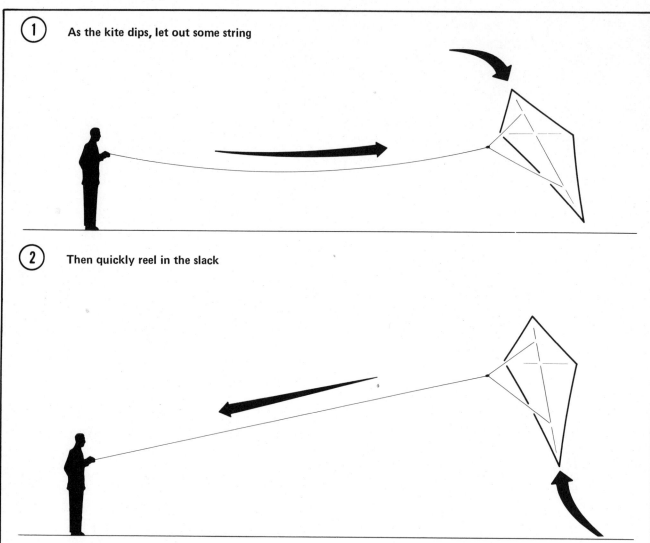

① As the kite dips, let out some string

② Then quickly reel in the slack

(1) In the winching process, the kite-flyer lets out a little line as the kite starts to fall, and (2) then quickly reels in just before the kite touches the ground, causing the kite to soar upward.

With the winching method you still launch the kite as before, but as it starts to fall you let out a little more line. Then just before the kite touches the ground, quickly reel in the string. That should cause the kite to soar. When it reaches the utmost height it can attain and starts to float back down, let out more line. Before it reaches the ground, however, pull sharply on the line; that will cause the kite to climb again. This process can be repeated until the kite reaches a satisfactory altitude where the wind will support it.

In all kite-launching, you must take care not to let the line out too quickly or else the kite will fall. The amount of line to release depends on the type and size of the kite you are flying as well as the wind conditions. Generally speaking, the stronger the wind, the more flying line that you can release.

Controlling The Kite In Flight

YOU CAN ALSO help your kite rise during flight by pulling on the flying line. If the kite does not rise, most likely the bridle needs adjustment. On a flat kite, for example, a bridle positioned too low may make the kite fly at too vertical an angle rather than at the proper 45-degree angle. If this is the case, try moving the bridle ring toward the top of the kite.

On the other hand, a bridle ring that is too high may make the kite continually flutter and dip. The reason it does so is that the kite is flying on too flat a plane in the wind. If you

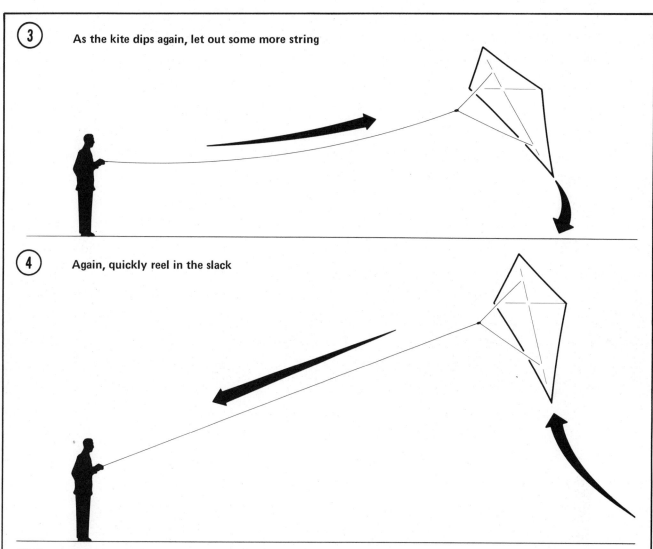

③ **As the kite dips again, let out some more string**

④ **Again, quickly reel in the slack**

(3) Continuing the winching process, the kite-flyer again lets out line when the kite drifts down, and (4) then pulls sharply to get the kite up to where the wind will support it.

notice your kite fluttering and dipping, merely move the bridle ring down toward the center of the kite.

If the kite not only dips but does loops as well, you can assume that a longer tail is needed. A shorter tail is indicated if the tail hangs straight downward instead of flowing out behind the kite or if the tail noticeably restricts the kite's movement.

If the kite suddenly dives to one side in flight, you can regain control by quickly releasing more line. If the kite drifts slowly to the left or to the right, however, you must run it across the wind in the same direction. A kite that repeatedly falls to the left or the right, though, may be suffering from a bridle ring that is not centered properly. If the kite repeatedly falls to

the right, try moving the bridle ring a little to the left; if the kite falls to the left, move it right.

Once the kite is flying, you cannot simply sit back and relax. The wind is constantly changing and you must make adjustments to keep the kite flying well.

Naturally, every kite has its flight limits and conditions; these limits and conditions are dependent on the type of kite it is and on the wind conditions on a particular day. Suppose you see excess sag in the flying line. You conclude that the kite can no longer support the line, and you can either accept this limit or you can compensate by forming a "kite train," i.e., attaching another kite to the line.

To create a kite train, first reel in the excess line and eliminate the sag. Then launch another kite on at least 100 feet of flying line and attach this line to the main line that you were using. You have now increased the total lifting surface significantly. Do not forget, however, that you have also greatly increased the pull on the kite line. Be sure, therefore, that your flying line and bridle are strong enough to handle the increased tension. A well-constructed kite train flown in the right wind conditions can soar to very high altitudes.

The last step in effective kite flying involves retrieving the kite. When the time comes to bring down the kite, keep one thing in mind: Do it slowly. This is the time when the kite encounters the strongest air resistance and that means it is the time when the kite faces the greatest danger of being damaged.

In a gentle wind, you can merely reel the kite in. Just make sure that no one is standing in the path of the kite as you bring it in. In a stronger wind, you may have to walk toward the kite as you reel it in. If the kite starts to loop and appears as though it may crash as it nears the ground, get ready to under-run the kite in order to bring it down. This is done by having a helper hold the reel as you place your gloved hand over the line and walk toward the kite, keeping the line parallel to the ground. After walking a reasonable distance, stop, turn around, and walk back toward your helper who reels in the line that you bring down. Repeat this under-run process until the kite has gradually been brought down.

When the kite nears the ground, it is better to drop the string and let the kite float rather than risk dragging it across the ground.

Bringing down a box kite can often present an extraordinary challenge because box kites tend to drop suddenly when they are reeled in. It may be advisable to have your helper try to catch the box kite as it descends in order to prevent it from crashing.

Above all, remember not to rush the landing process. Your primary concern is to bring the kite in safely so that you can have the pleasure of flying it again.

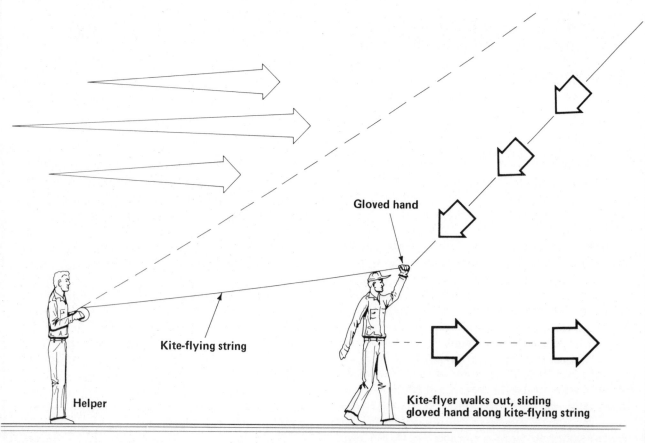

Gloved hand

Kite-flying string

Helper

Kite-flyer walks out, sliding gloved hand along kite-flying string

To under-run a kite, the flyer walks toward the kite with a gloved hand on the line while the helper holds the reel.

The Diamond Kite

FLAT OR PLANE kites date back to the earliest kites made in China. Today they rank among the easier kites to construct, although they lend themselves to a wide variety of shapes and sizes. The number of framing sticks — or spars, as they are called in the jargon of aerodynamics — will differ according to the type of flat kite being constructed.

The classic diamond kite is probably the most familiar kite shape in North America; it is the one most often seen in parks on a spring day, and it is the one most often found on store shelves. The diamond kite is not as maneuverable as some other kites, although it can fly at relatively greater heights and withstand stronger winds than many other designs.

The following directions for creating a flat diamond-shaped kite provide measurements in terms of proportion because you can con-

struct this type of kite in a wide range of sizes. Keep in mind, however, that to achieve optimum flight stability it is advisable to build a kite that is at least three feet long or wide.

Kite Frame Materials

YOU WILL NEED two spars, or dowels, to form the frame of the diamond kite. Select slender wooden sticks of cypress, spruce, or pine, or else use whitewood dowels. All these woods are both strong and lightweight — an important combination in all kite-making mate-

---

Editor's Note: The numbers and detail citations that appear in brackets [ ] throughout this chapter refer to the scale drawing of The Diamond Kite.

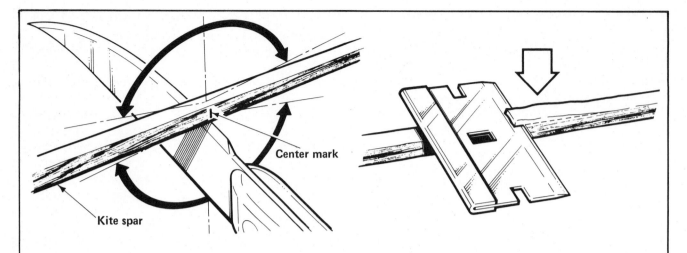

Balance each spar on a knife blade's edge.

Trim the spar's heavier side until it balances.

rials. You can obtain what you need at most hobby stores, lumber shops, and hardware stores.

Of the two spars, one should be exactly two-thirds the length of the other. Use the longer spar for the kite's centerpole [1], and the shorter spar to form the crossbar [2].

How To Create A Diamond Kite

ONCE YOU HAVE spars of the proper proportions, you must test them for balance. Mark the exact center of the length of each spar, and then balance each spar at its center mark on the edge of a knife blade. If one side of the spar tends to go down, you must correct the imbalance by whittling or sandpapering the heavier side until the spar balances properly.

Now take a sharp knife or saw and cut a notch in each end of both spars. These notches will later hold the guideline string [4]. Be careful, though, because notching can cause the wood to split if too much pressure is applied. To prevent splitting, lash the spar just below the notch.

You are now ready to join the two spars — the centerpole [1] and the crossbar [2]. Join them at the center of the crossbar [2], one-fourth the way down from the top of the centerpole [1]. Lay the spars in position, and then lash them together by taking at least two turns through both diagonals of the point of juncture [3]. The type of string you use for this purpose is not critical; an eight-inch length of common four-ply cotton string is quite suitable. On the

other hand, the string must be strong, non-stretching, and light enough that it does not add extra bulk to the construction. Weave the string over and under the juncture [3] and tie it with a square knot. Clip off any extra string.

Now test again for balance. It is very important that the kite frame be balanced on either side of the centerpole [1]. In order to test for balance, lay one end of the centerpole

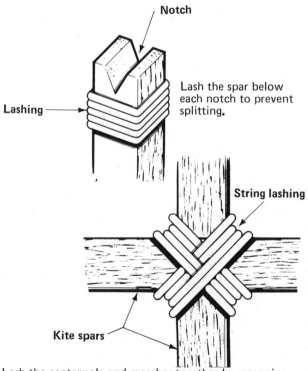

Notch

Lashing

Lash the spar below each notch to prevent splitting.

String lashing

Kite spars

Lash the centerpole and crossbar together by wrapping string through their point of juncture.

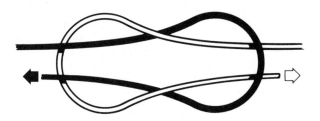

After lashing, tie the string ends into a square knot.

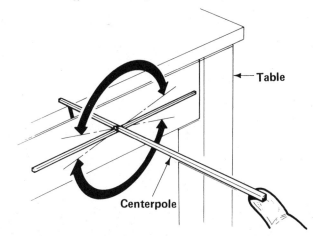

Test the entire kite frame for balance.

[1] on the edge of a table, and place the other end on the tip of your finger. The entire frame should rest along a horizontal plane. If the frame tends to dip to one side, you must correct the imbalance before proceeding any further in the construction. First check the centerpole [1] to make sure that it actually intersects the center of the crossbar [2]. If it does not, adjust the string until it is exactly centered. Then, if the imbalance persists, the cause must be an unequal weight of the sides of the crossbar [2]. Pare down the heavier side until the frame balances properly.

When you are satisfied that the frame balances, apply glue to the string. Any glue that dries quickly and becomes tough rather than brittle is appropriate for this job; but be sure to use enough glue to soak the string of the joints and knots thoroughly.

Now set the kite frame aside and allow it to dry. When it is dry, you will have a strong, balanced frame on which to construct a diamond kite.

The next step involves framing the centerpole [1] and crossbar [2] guideline string [4]. The purpose of the guideline string [4] is to provide a firm edge on which to mount the kite

cover and, of course, help the kite maintain its shape. You can use the same type of string for this guideline [4] that you used to lash the joints.

Attach the guideline string [4] to the notch at the top of the centerpole [1] by knotting it. Then guide the guideline string [4] to the notch in the crossbar [2], keeping the string taut at all times; knot the guideline string [4] to the crossbar in the same manner you knotted it to the centerpole [1]. Continue on around the frame, always keeping the string taut and the knots secure, until you have completely framed the kite. Then tie the two ends of the guideline string [4] together.

Preparing The Kite Cover

YOU ARE NOW ready to prepare the covering for the kite. Select a covering material that is both lightweight and strong; remember that the wind must not be able to blow through the kite cover material. Paper is the most popular material used to cover the diamond kite, although a lightweight fabric also works well. Any of the following types of paper are suitable for a diamond kite: wrapping paper, tissue paper, newspaper, shelf paper, brown paper, rice paper, or even the imitation Japanese paper found at art supply stores.

Place the kite frame on the kite covering [5], and then trace with a pencil around the outside edge of the frame (the guideline string [4]) leaving a half-inch margin around the entire kite. Later, you will glue this margin over the guideline string [4] frame. Now make additional markings on the kite covering [5] at each of the four points where the centerpole [1] and crossbar [2] will protrude. The covering, therefore, will be slightly smaller than the actual frame at these points.

Once the pattern is properly traced on the covering [5], cut it out with sharp scissors. At this point, it is time to decorate the kite. If you wish to paint the kite covering [5], you can choose from among watercolors, poster paints, and water-thinned acrylic colors, but keep in mind that the paint must dry quickly and must be flexible and lightweight. For suggestions and tips on how to decorate the kite, refer to the chapter "Decorating the Kite."

Now position the frame over the undecorated side of the kite covering [5] with the crossbar [2] against the covering [5] and the centerpole [1] above it. Crease the margin of

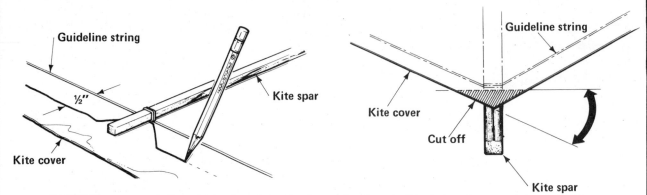

(LEFT) Trace around the outside edge of the kite frame, leaving a half-inch margin around the entire kite.
(RIGHT) Make additional marks on the kite cover where the centerpole and crossbar will protrude.

the covering [5] over the guideline string frame [4], apply glue to the margin, and then seal the margin securely with the guideline string [4] inside. Work slowly and try to avoid wrinkles and creases. If you use fabric for the kite covering, you can either glue it or sew it with a running stitch around the guideline string frame [4]. Wait until the glue is completely dry before proceeding to the next step.

You must now prepare a bridle which is necessary to control the angle at which the surface of the kite meets the wind. Begin by cutting a piece of string equal in length to the length of the centerpole [1] added to the length of the crossbar [2]. Knot one end of the string to the top of the spine. Then loop the bridle string [6] two or three times through a bridle ring — a curtain ring will suffice — at a position a little higher than the halfway point on the bridle string [6]. Tie the other end of the bridle

string [6] to the bottom of the kite centerpole [1].

Next, cut a second piece of string equal to twice the width of the crossbar [2]. Attach one end of this bridle string [7] to one end of the crossbar [2], loop it two or three times through the bridle ring, and then tie the bridle string [7] to the other end of the crossbar [2].

The bridle ring should be above the center of the kite; you can adjust it by sliding it along the bridle strings [6 and 7]. When the ring is adjusted properly, you can wrap a small piece of adhesive tape around the ring to hold the bridle strings [6 and 7] secure. Do nothing, however, to make this position more permanent because you may wish to adjust the bridle ring in the future to accommodate varying wind conditions.

The final step in the construction of a diamond kite is to fashion a tail [8] [Detail A]. All flat kites must have a tail, which provides stability both by its weight and its air resistance. You will need a strip of cloth [8] approximately twice the length of the centerpole [1] and short strips [9] to be attached at six-inch intervals along the tail strip [8]. Secure the short strips [9] by knotting them to the tail [8] every six inches; the knots must be tight enough to prevent the strips [9] from sliding down the tail [8] when the kite is in flight.

Finally, tie or tape one end of the tail [8] to the bottom of the centerpole, and the kite is ready to fly. You may find that the tail needs further adjustment depending on the wind conditions. If the kite tends to loop and spin in flight, it needs a longer tail. On the other hand, if the tail seems to restrict the movement of the kite, shorten it somewhat.

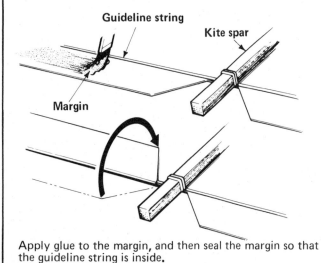

Apply glue to the margin, and then seal the margin so that the guideline string is inside.

The Diamond Kite

Scale: Grid Squares = ½"

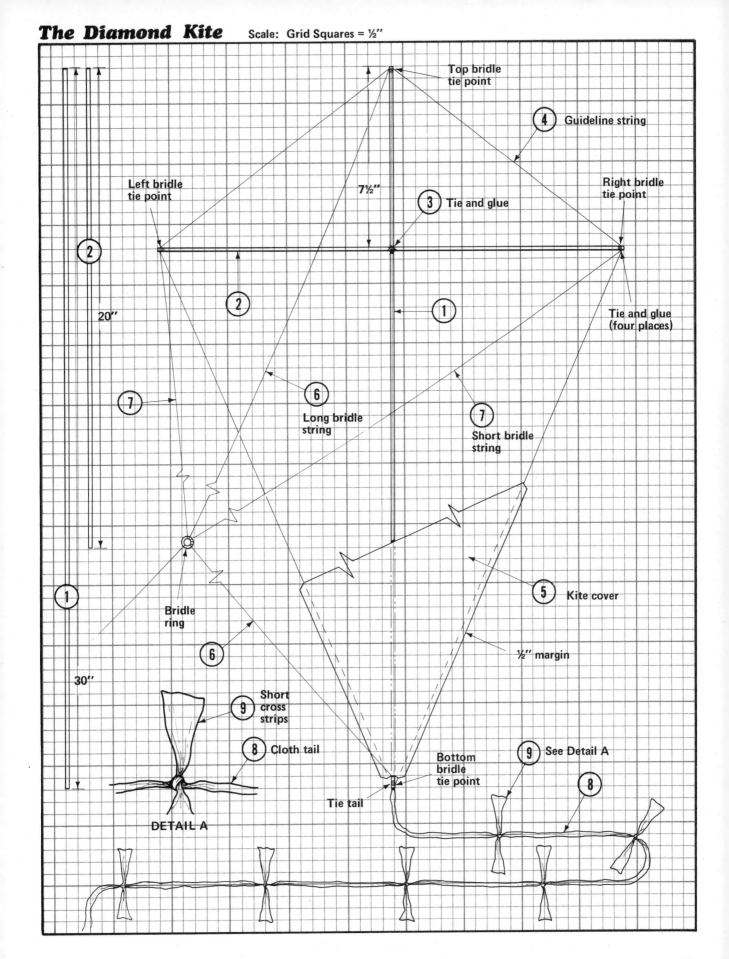

Top bridle tie point

④ Guideline string

Left bridle tie point

7½"

③ Tie and glue

Right bridle tie point

② Tie and glue (four places)

20"

②

①

⑦

⑥ Long bridle string

⑦ Short bridle string

① Bridle ring

⑤ Kite cover

⑥

½" margin

30"

⑨ Short cross strips

⑧ Cloth tail

⑨ See Detail A

Bottom bridle tie point

Tie tail

⑧

DETAIL A

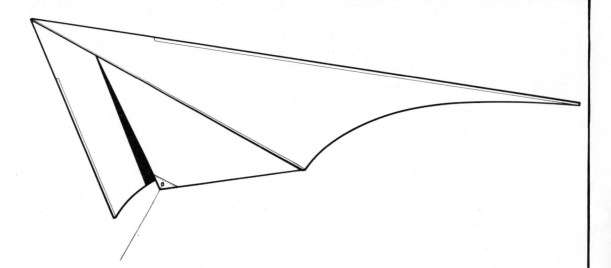

The Delta Kite

COMPARED TO some of the kites that have their roots in antiquity, the delta kite is a very modern design. It is one of the most popular kites, essentially because it is easy to construct and because it flies extremely well. The basic delta kite is simply an isosceles triangle — one that has two sides equal — with a keel for stability.

The directions that follow are for a typical delta kite of average size. You can, of course, make much larger versions as long as you maintain the proper proportions.

Kite Frame Materials

TO CONSTRUCT the frame of the delta kite, you will need four spars — either slender wooden sticks of pine or spruce or pre-fashioned whitewood dowels. These woods which are both strong and lightweight are usually available at hobby shops, lumber markets, and hardware stores. If you want to make a very large kite, substitute aluminum tubing for the wood.

You will need two 36-inch spars to form the wings [1], one 29-inch spar for the centerpole [2], and one 24¼-inch spar for the cross-spar support [3]. When the wing spars [1], centerpole [2], and cross-spar support [3] are cut to the proper length, you are ready to proceed directly to the preparation of the cover.

Preparing The Kite Cover

A LIGHTWEIGHT but sturdy cloth, like nylon, is the ideal choice for the wing kite cover [4]. Light cotton, plastic sheeting, Tyvek, half-mil Mylar, sailcloth, and even polyethylene bagging also work quite well. Just make sure that the covering you select is both lightweight and strong.

The first thing to do is make a paper pattern for the wing kite cover [4]. Draw a line 66 inches long to form the base of the triangle, and then make a pencil mark 29 inches above the exact center of this line. Next, draw connecting lines between this mark and each end of the line to form a triangular pattern. You must now add a half-inch margin to the two outside wings that extends 36 inches up from the base line; the margin thus stops eight inches from the tip of the triangle. These margins are to form the pockets [5] that will hold the wing spars [1].

Now lay the paper pattern on the covering material, and trace around it with a pencil.

Editor's Note: The numbers and detail citations that appear in brackets [ ] throughout this chapter refer to the scale drawing of The Delta Kite.

Then carefully cut out the wing kite cover [4] with sharp scissors. Before proceeding any further, fold the cover in half to make absolutely certain that both sides (which will extend out on either side of the keel [6]) are identical. Make the appropriate adjustment — if any — as needed to create a perfectly symmetrical wing kite cover [4].

You are now ready to prepare the keel [6] for the delta kite. Use the same material that you used for the wing kite cover [4] and you would also be wise to start with a paper pattern before cutting out the actual keel [6].

The keel [6], like the wings [4], is triangular in shape. Draw a line 23 inches long for the base of this triangle, and then make a pencil mark at a position that is exactly eight inches in from the left side of the line and eight inches directly above the line. This mark designates the tip of the triangle. Now draw lines connecting this dot to each end of the base line. One side of the triangle should be 11½ inches long, and the other side should be 17 inches long. Finally, place this pattern on the actual material you are using for the keel [6], and trace and cut as you did the wing kite cover [4].

Now you can join the wing kite cover [4] and the keel [6] together [Detail A]. First, fold the wing kite cover [4] evenly along its center from top to bottom. Place the long base line of the keel [6] — leading edge forward — inside this fold. Next, either stitch or glue these three thicknesses together from top to bottom about ⅜ of an inch from the crease. If the kite material is plastic, you can either insert the 29-inch centerpole [2] within this fold before gluing or attach it with tape [7] after the glue is dry. If you are using fabric, you can simply insert the centerpole [2] after stitching the seam; but whatever material you use, be sure to avoid wrinkling or creasing it while joining the wing kite cover [4] and the keel [6].

Once the centerpole [2] is permanently attached to the wing kite cover [4], you can attach the wing spars [1]. If you are working with a fabric wing kite cover [4], fold the margin over and sew a running stitch to form pockets [5] for the wing spars on both sides. Then insert a 36-inch wing spar [1] in each pocket [5] and close the ends permanently by stitching or stapling. If the wing kite cover [4] is plastic, you should enclose the wing spars [1] in the margin and seal the pockets [5] securely with glue or tape [7]. These three spars — centerpole [2] and the two wing spars [1] — constitute the permanent frame of the delta kite.

If you have not already decorated the kite cover material, now is the time to do so. If you wish to paint the kite covering, use watercolors, poster paints, or water-thinned acrylic colors. Keep in mind, however, that the paint or coloring you use must be flexible, lightweight, and quick-drying.

The shape of a delta kite lends itself well to representations of a bat, a stingray, or a butterfly; it can, of course, be decorated less realistically with abstract forms. For suggestions and tips on how to decorate the kite, refer to the chapter "Decorating The Kite"; for ideas, examine the full-color illustration of The Delta Kite.

The next step in the preparation of a delta kite is to attach the cross-spar support [3]. Spread the delta kite out flat with the keel [6] underneath so that you can attach the cross-spar support [3] to the back side of the kite.

Measure from the front tip of the kite to a point 12 inches down the centerpole [2]. The two ends of the cross-spar support [3] are to be attached just inside the wing spars [1] along this 12-inch point. Now drill a pilot hole in each end of the cross-spar support [3], and screw metal hooks [8] (small drapery hooks work well) into these holes. Then lash the ends of the cross-spar support [3] with string to hold the hooks securely [Detail B].

Next, make holes for eyelets [9] in each wing kite cover [4] just inside the wing spar [1], apply small pieces of cloth tape [7] to these points for reinforcement, and sink the eyelets [9] through both the tape [7] and the wing kite cover [4]. Finally, insert the cross-spar support hooks [8] into the wing kite cover eyelets [9]. The whole idea of this construction is to create a joint between the cross-spar support [3] and the wing kite cover [4] that is highly flexible.

The last step is to attach a kite flying line [10] to the keel [6]. Make a hole in the keel [6] just behind its triangular tip, reinforce the hole with cloth tape, and put an eyelet [9] through this reinforced hole. Tie the kite flying line to the keel [6] by guiding it through the eyelet [9] and then knotting it.

Because the delta kite is not rigid, it is self-adjusting. Consequently, it does not need a tail as long as it is properly balanced. The delta kite flies well under most circumstances, but it is at its best in light to moderate wind velocities.

The Delta Kite

Scale: Grid Squares = 1"

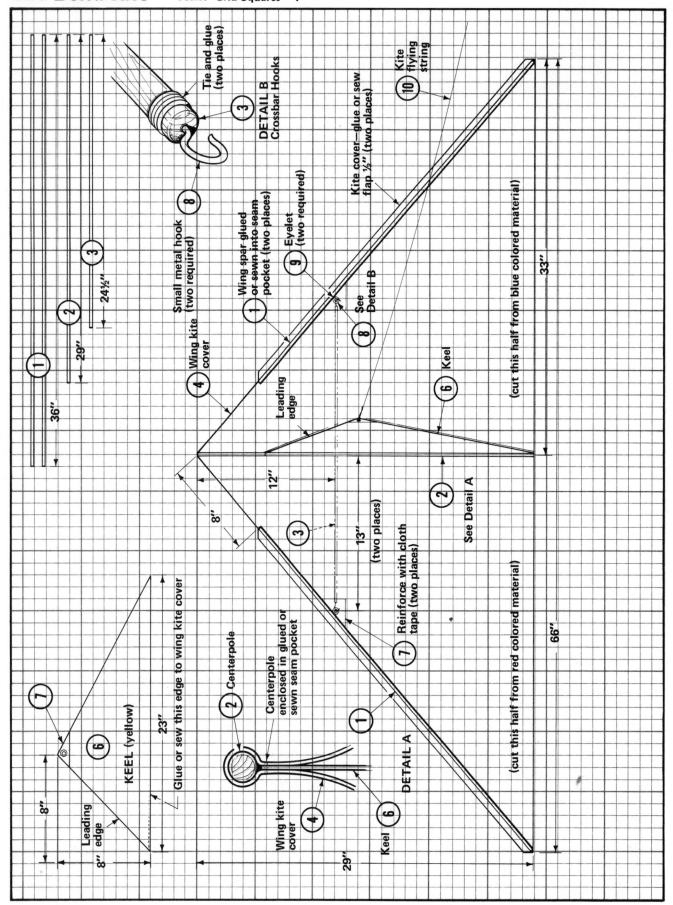

Tie and glue (two places)

③

DETAIL B
Crossbar Hooks

⑧

Small metal hook (two required)

④ Wing kite cover

① Wing spar glued or sewn into seam pocket (two places)

⑨ Eyelet (two required)

⑧ See Detail B

Leading edge

36"

29"

24½"

① ② ③

12"

8"

13" (two places)

③

① ② ③

Kite cover—glue or sew flap ½" (two places)

⑩ Kite flying string

33"

66"

(cut this half from blue colored material)

⑥ Keel

② See Detail A

⑦ Reinforce with cloth tape (two places)

KEEL (yellow)

23"

Glue or sew this edge to wing kite cover

② Centerpole

Centerpole enclosed in glued or sewn seam pocket

Wing kite cover

④

⑥ Keel

① ⑦ ⑥

DETAIL A

Leading edge

8"

8"

8"

29"

(cut this half from red colored material)

34

The Malay Kite

THE MALAY KITE, named for the Asian peninsula where it was first popular, is the most popular of the bowed kites. Flown for centuries in almost all regions of Asia, the Malay kite did not make its mark in the western world until the late 1800's when the famous showman/photographer/kite-inventor William Eddy introduced it. Since then, it has been used by the United States Weather Bureau to gather meteorological information and by the United States Army during World War II to serve as a gunnery target.

The Malay kite, or the Eddy kite as it is often called today, flies quite well in tandem. It is basically a two-spar kite with a T-shape frame, differing from the familiar flat diamond kite essentially in its bowed crossbar. This bowing makes the Malay kite self-stabilizing, both horizontally and vertically. Another distinguishing characteristic of the Malay kite is its lack of a tail; a tail is not necessary on a properly constructed bowed kite because the bowing itself stabilizes the kite in flight.

The following directions for creating a Malay kite provide measurements in terms of proportion because you can construct this type of kite in a wide range of sizes. You should, however, build it with spars that are at least three feet long in order to achieve optimum flight stability.

Editor's Note: The numbers and detail citations that appear in brackets [ ] throughout this chapter refer to the scale drawing of The Malay Kite.

Kite Frame Materials

YOU NEED TWO spars or dowels of equal length to form the frame of the Malay kite. One spar forms the centerpole [1] of the kite, while the other spar forms the crossbar [2]. Slender wooden sticks of cypress, spruce, or pine will make satisfactory spars, as will whitewood dowels. These woods are both strong and lightweight, necessary characteristics for kite frame spars. You can obtain these woods easily at most hobby stores, lumber shops, and hardware stores.

How To Create A Malay Kite

AFTER CUTTING the centerpole [1] and crossbar [2] to their proper lengths, you must test them for balance. An important requirement for any successful kite, proper balance is particularly crucial for the Malay kite. Test for balance by marking the centerpole [1] and crossbar [2] at their exact centers. Then place each one on the edge of a knife blade at its center mark. If one side tends to go down, the spar [1 or 2] is not balanced, and you must correct the imbalance by whittling or sandpapering the heavier side until it balances as it should.

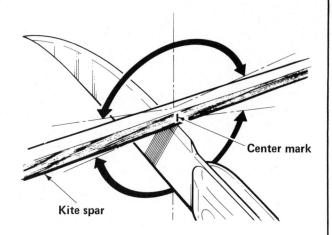

Test the spars for balance by marking their exact centers and placing them at their center points on the edge of a knife blade.

When both the centerpole [1] and crossbar [2] balance, cut notches in both ends of each one. Later, these notches will hold the guideline string [3]. You can cut the notches with either a sharp knife or a saw, but you must reinforce the notches to prevent the wood from

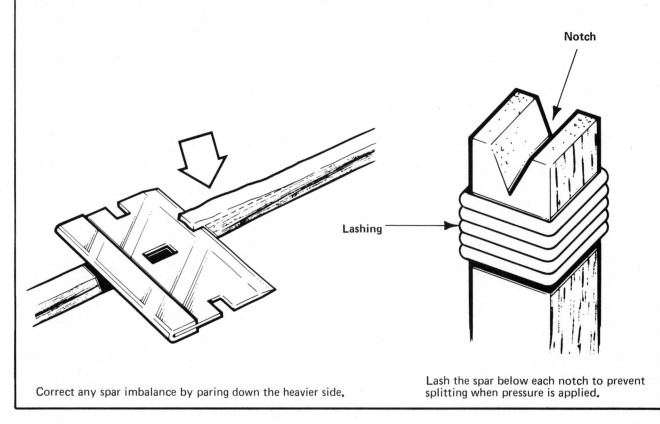

Correct any spar imbalance by paring down the heavier side.

Lash the spar below each notch to prevent splitting when pressure is applied.

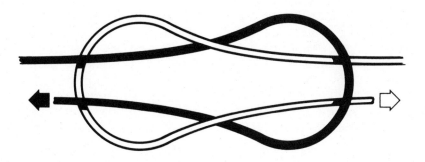

Join the ends of the string used for lashing the center pole and crossbar into a square knot and clip off any excess string.

splitting when pressure is applied. Therefore, lash each end of the centerpole [1] and crossbar [2] just below the notches.

You are now ready to join the centerpole [1] and the crossbar [2]. The point of juncture should be at the exact center of the crossbar [2], one-fifth of the way down from the top of the centerpole [1]. First, lay the spars [1 and 2] in the proper position. Next, lash them together by wrapping a piece of string at least eight inches long a minimum of two turns through both diagonals of the point of juncture. The type of string for this purpose is not critical; a common four-ply cotton string is quite suitable. The only requirements are that it be strong, non-stretching, and non-bulky. Weave the string over and under the point of juncture, tie it with a square knot, and clip off any excess string.

Now test the entire kite frame for balance by laying one end of the centerpole [1] on the edge of a table and placing the other end on the tip of your finger. The frame should rest along a horizontal plane. If the frame tends to dip to one side, you must correct the imbalance before proceeding any further in the construction.

To correct the imbalance, first check to be sure that the centerpole [1] actually intersects the exact center of the crossbar [2]. If it does not, adjust the string until it does. If the frame still fails to balance, the cause is probably due

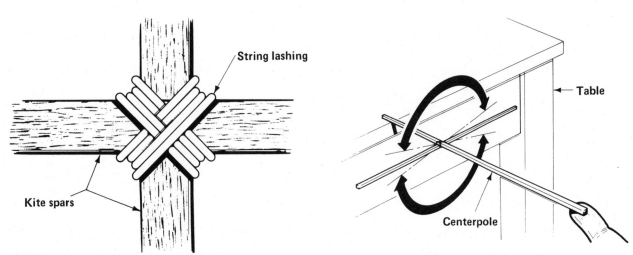

(LEFT) Lash the centerpole and crossbar together by wrapping a piece of string through both diagonals of the point of juncture. (RIGHT) Test the kite frame for balance by resting one end of the centerpole on the edge of a table and the other end on the tip of your finger.

to an unequal weight of the sides of the crossbar [2]. Whittle or sandpaper the heavier side of the crossbar [2] until the frame balances as it should.

When you are satisfied that the frame balances, soak the string and knot at the point of juncture thoroughly with glue. Any glue that dries quickly and becomes tough rather than brittle is appropriate for this job. Be sure that you use enough glue, however, to soak the string and knot thoroughly.

Now set the kite frame aside and allow it to dry. When it is dry, you will have a strong, balanced frame on which to construct a Malay kite.

The next step is to frame the centerpole [1] and crossbar [2] with a guideline string [3]. The guideline string [3] will provide a firm edge on which to mount the kite cover as well as help the kite maintain its shape during flight. Use the same type of string that you used to lash the joint for this guideline string [3]. Attach it to the notch at the top of the centerpole [1] by knotting it, and then run the guideline string [3] to one of the notches in the crossbar [2]. Keep the guideline string [3] taut at all times, and attach it to the crossbar [2] the same way you attached it to the centerpole [1] — by knotting it. Continue on around the frame, always keeping the guideline string [3] taut and the knots secure, until you have framed the kite completely. Then tie the two ends of the guideline string [3] together without permitting any slack to occur.

Preparing The Kite Cover

YOU ARE NOW ready to prepare the kite cover [4]. Select a covering material that is lightweight but strong. Remember, the wind must not be able to blow through the cover material. Fabric is best because it is flexible. Lightweight fabric like cotton cambric makes an excellent cover material for this Malay kite. When the kite is bowed, moreover, the pocketing of the lightweight fabric over the frame will promote stability. On the other hand, strong papers like tissue paper, crepe paper, shelf paper, and wrapping paper are also quite suitable.

Place the kite frame on the kite cover [4], and, with a pencil, trace around the outside edge of the frame (the guideline string [3]), leaving a half-inch margin around the entire kite. Later, you will glue or sew this margin to overlap the string frame.

Now, notch the corners of the kite cover [4] pattern to allow for turning at the four points where the centerpole [1] and crossbar [2] will protrude. Once you have the frame pattern properly traced on the covering material, cut it out with sharp scissors to create the kite cover [4] itself.

At this point, with the kite cover [4] cut to size, it is time to decorate. If you wish to paint the kite cover [4], use watercolors, poster paints, or water-thinned acrylic colors; just keep in mind that the paint must be lightweight, dry quickly, and remain flexible when

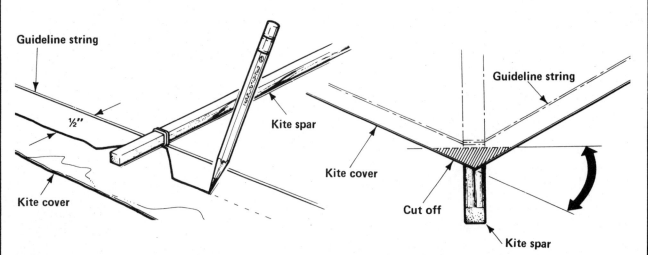

Guideline string

½"

Kite spar

Kite cover

Kite cover

Guideline string

Kite cover

Cut off

Kite spar

(LEFT) Place the kite frame on the kite cover and trace around the guideline string, leaving a half-inch margin around the entire frame. (RIGHT) Notch the corners of the kite cover to allow for turning at the four points where the centerpole and crossbar will protrude.

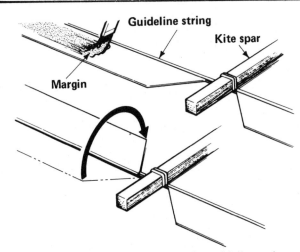

Crease the margin of the cover over the guideline string frame, apply glue, and seal securely with guideline inside.

dry. For suggestions, tips, and ideas regarding the Malay kite decoration, refer to the chapter "Decorating the Kite" and to the full-color illustration of the Malay Kite.

Now position the frame over the undecorated side of the kite cover [4] with the crossbar [2] against the cover [4] and the centerpole [1] above it. Crease the margin of the kite cover [4] over the guideline string [3] frame, apply glue, and seal the margin securely with the guideline string [3] inside. If you selected fabric for the kite cover [4], you can either glue or stitch it with a running stitch. In either case, work slowly and try to avoid any wrinkles or creases. If you glue the kite cover [4] to the frame, wait until the glue is com-

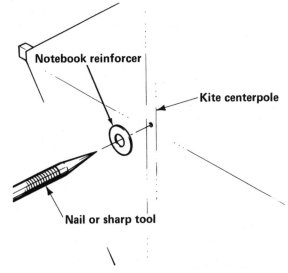

Punch holes in the kite cover to accommodate the bridle string; be sure to apply a notebook reinforcer around each hole to prevent tearing.

pletely dry before proceeding to the next step.

You must now prepare either a one-legged or two-legged bridle; the bridle controls the angle at which the surface of the Malay kite meets the wind. The two-legged bridle is the one that is used most often, and it is the one described here.

First, cut a piece of bridle string [5] equal in length to 1½ times the length of the centerpole [1]. Next, with a nail or sharp-pointed tool, carefully make a hole in the kite cover [4] just at the point where the centerpole [1] and crossbar [2] intersect. If the kite cover [4] is made of paper, apply a notebook reinforcer to the hole to prevent tearing. Now guide one end of the bridle string [5] through the hole you just made, and tie it securely to the frame. Loop the other end of the bridle string [5] two or three times through a bridle ring (a curtain ring can be used for this purpose), and then tie this end of the bridle string [5] securely to the bottom of the centerpole [1]. Adjust the placement of the bridle ring by sliding it along the bridle string [5] until it is about one-fifth of the way down from the top of the bridle string [5]. Further adjustment of the bridle ring may be necessary after test-flying the kite, depending upon the strength of the wind.

The final step before actually launching your Malay kite is to bow the kite — that is, to bend the crossbar [2] of the kite backwards so that it forms a bow [Detail A]. Cut a piece of string [6] 56 inches in length. Tie one end of the string [6] securely to one end of the crossbar [2]. Then take the other end of the string [6], and tie it securely to the other end of the crossbar [2], bowing the crossbar so that it assumes the proper degree of bow. Generally, you bow the crossbar [2] approximately one tenth of its total length — or, in this case, about 4¾ inches. You would be wise to release this bowing when you are not flying the kite in order to preserve the tautness of the crossbar [2] and to facilitate transporting and storing your Malay kite.

Your Malay kite is now ready to fly; no tail is necessary since the dihedral effect produced by the bowing creates a self-correcting kite. Pockets formed when the wind strikes the covering stabilize the airborne Malay kite. In addition, the Malay kite enjoys good lift because it is short and wide, and its comparatively low weight in relation to its surface area makes it a highly efficient flying device.

The Malay Kite Scale: Grid Squares = 1″

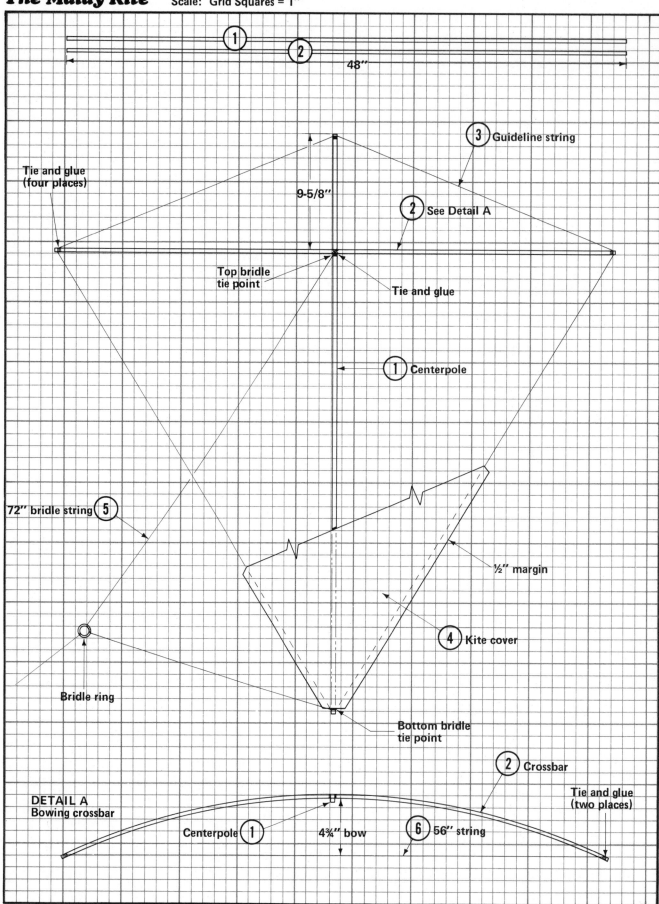

①

②

48″

③ Guideline string

Tie and glue
(four places)

9-5/8″

② See Detail A

Top bridle
tie point

Tie and glue

① Centerpole

72″ bridle string ⑤

½″ margin

④ Kite cover

Bridle ring

Bottom bridle
tie point

② Crossbar

Tie and glue
(two places)

DETAIL A
Bowing crossbar

Centerpole ①

4¾″ bow

⑥ 56″ string

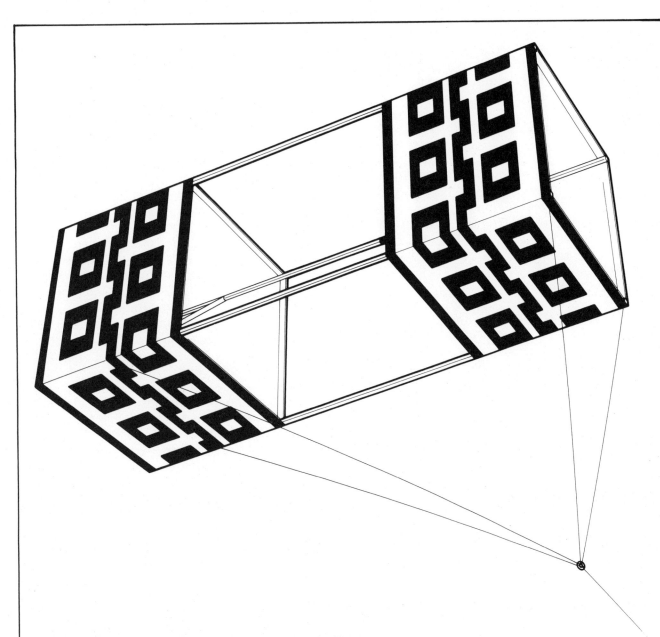

The Box Kite

THE BASIC box kite, now a familiar sight wherever kites are flown, did not come on the scene until 1892. Invented that year by Lawrence Hargrave, it was the first of the cellular kites, and it represented a major change in kite design.

The box kite, although modified to some extent over the years, still remains basically a box shape. The frame is formed by four upright spars at equal distances from each other and wrapped with two separate panels of covering. The frame is supported by X-shaped cross-spars.

The measurements that follow are meant

Editor's Note: The numbers and detail citations that appear in brackets [ ] throughout this chapter refer to the scale drawing of The Box Kite.

to indicate an average size box kite; you can make one considerably larger, provided that you maintain the proper proportions and use materials that have adequate strength for the larger dimensions.

Kite Frame Materials

YOU WILL NEED four 40-inch upright spars [1] and four 17-inch cross-spars [2]. Slender wooden spars of cypress, spruce, or pine or whitewood dowels work well; these woods combine both strength and lightness, and they are available at most hobby stores, lumber shops, or hardware stores.

How To Create A Box Kite

WHEN YOU FINISH cutting the spars to their proper length, you must test the four upright spars [1] for balance. Draw a pencil line at the midpoint of each upright spar [1], and then place this center mark on the edge of a knife blade. If the upright spar [1] fails to hover on a horizontal plane, then it is not balanced. Correct the imbalance by whittling or sandpapering the heavier side, the one that tends to go down, until the upright spar [1] balances as it should. Then follow the same procedure for all four upright spars [1].

Now take two of the 17-inch cross-spars [2], and, using a sharp knife, cut notches in both ends of each one [Detail A]. The notched ends will fit around the four upright spars [1] when you assemble the kite. Then lash the spars just below the notching.

Next, mark the exact center of each cross-spar [2], and then carefully cut notches at those points so that the cross-spars [2] will fit tightly together, forming an "X" with exact 90-degree angles. Lash the cross-spars [2] together with string at this point of juncture, taking at least two turns through both diagonals of the joint. Use strong string that will not stretch or add bulk; common four-ply cotton string is quite suitable for this purpose. Then weave the string over and under the sticks, and tie the string with a square knot. Clip off any excess string. Repeat this lashing process with the other two cross-spars [2].

You must now test the balance of each set of cross-spars. Place one end of a cross-spar [2] on the edge of a table and the other end of the same cross-spar [2] on the tip of your finger. The entire frame should rest along a horizontal plane, and if it dips to one side, you know you have a balance problem which must be corrected before you can proceed any further in the construction. To correct the balance, first check to be sure that the point of cross-spar [2] juncture is located at the exact center marking of each cross-spar [2]. If it is not, adjust the string until the cross-spars [2] are centered exactly. If that is not the source of

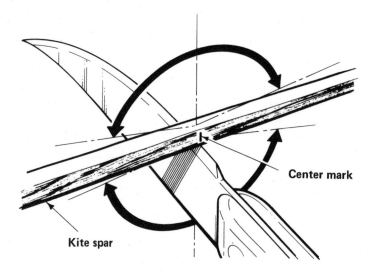

Center mark

Kite spar

To test a spar for balance, make a mark at its center point and then place this center mark on the edge of a knife blade.

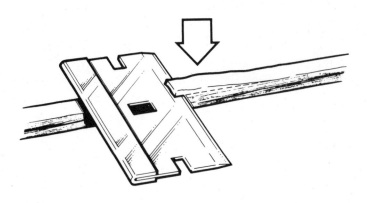

Pare down the heavier side of a spar until it balances as it should.

the imbalance, you will probably find that a cross-spar [2] is heavier on one side than it is on the other. Whittle or sandpaper the heavier side until proper balance is achieved. Be sure to test the balance along both cross-spars [2] of the "X" on both sets of cross-spars [2].

When you are satisfied that both sets are balanced, apply glue to the lashings. Any glue that dries quickly and becomes tough rather than brittle is appropriate. Just make sure that you use enough glue to soak the string and the knots thoroughly. Then set the two sets of cross-spars [2] aside and allow them to dry completely.

Preparing The Kite Cover

THE NEXT STEP is to prepare the kite cover [3]. A box kite is usually covered with lightweight cloth; heavy-gauge Mylar, Tyvek, ripstop nylon, or even strong paper constitute good covering materials. You will need two strips of material, each one 12 x 50 inches, for this covering [3]. Cut the kite covering [3] to the proper measurements, and then mark each strip at 12-inch intervals, measuring from the left. The two inches remaining after the last mark will be used later for overlap.

Now position the kite cover strips [3] so

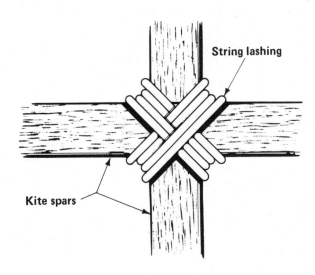

String lashing

Kite spars

Lash the cross-spars together at their point of juncture by weaving string over and under both diagonals of the joint.

that they are parallel and separated by a space of 16 inches [Detail C]. Then apply a neat line of glue to the markings denoting the first 12-inch interval on each kite cover [3]. Place one of the 40-inch upright spars [1] on the lines so that the kite cover [3] and the upright spar [1] are glued together securely. Repeat the same process for the three remaining upright spars [1] on the next three sets of lines. Make sure that both kite covers [3] remain exactly parallel, and wait until the glue dries completely before proceeding to the next step.

You now have a 12-inch flap remaining on one side of the kite cover [3] and a two-inch flap on the other side. Fold these flaps over so that the 12-inch flap overlaps the two-inch flap, and then glue the flaps together. Again wait until the glue dries before proceeding.

You are now ready to insert the cross-spar frames [2] six inches deep inside each cell of the box kite [Detail D]. The notched ends of the cross-spar frames [2] should fit snugly over the upright spars [1], creating a box shape that is 12 inches on each side. The cross-spar frames [2] will supply the rigidity required to maintain the kite's shape.

The final step is to add a bridle [Detail E]. The original (Hargrave) box kite design generally included only a single bridle. Now, however, a two-legged or four-legged bridle is considered more efficient.

To fashion a four-legged bridle, first use a nail or sharp-pointed tool to make a hole in the kite covering [3] of the top cell directly over the upright spar [1] and at the position of the cross-spar frame [2] — approximately six inches down from the top of the kite. Make another hole at this same position over the upright spar [1] across from the first one. If you are using paper for the kite covering [3], apply a notebook reinforcer around the holes to prevent tearing.

Next, cut a piece of bridle string [4] 50 inches long, and guide it through the first hole, tying it securely to the kite frame. Now take the other end of the bridle string [4], loop it two or three times through a bridle ring (a curtain ring works well), and then guide the bridle string [4] through the second hole, tying it rightly to the kite frame.

Finally, cut a piece of bridle string [5] about 60 inches long. Tie one end of the bridle string [5] to the bottom end of the same upright spar [1] to which you attached the first bridle

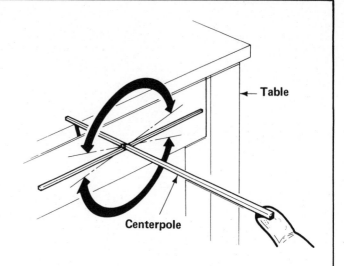

Test the entire kite frame for balance.

string [4]. Loop the bridle string [5] two or three times through the bridle ring, and then tie it securely to the bottom of the second upright spar [1] that you used.

Your box kite is now ready to fly. It will function well in moderate to strong winds. With a four-legged bridle, the box kite flies with a flat edge or lifting surface. With a two-legged bridle — attached at the same points but on only one upright spar [1] instead of two — the box kite flies at an angle, which results in less lift but even greater stability.

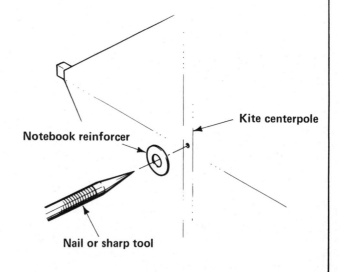

Punch holes in the kite cover for the bridle string.

The Box Kite   Scale: Grid Squares = 1"

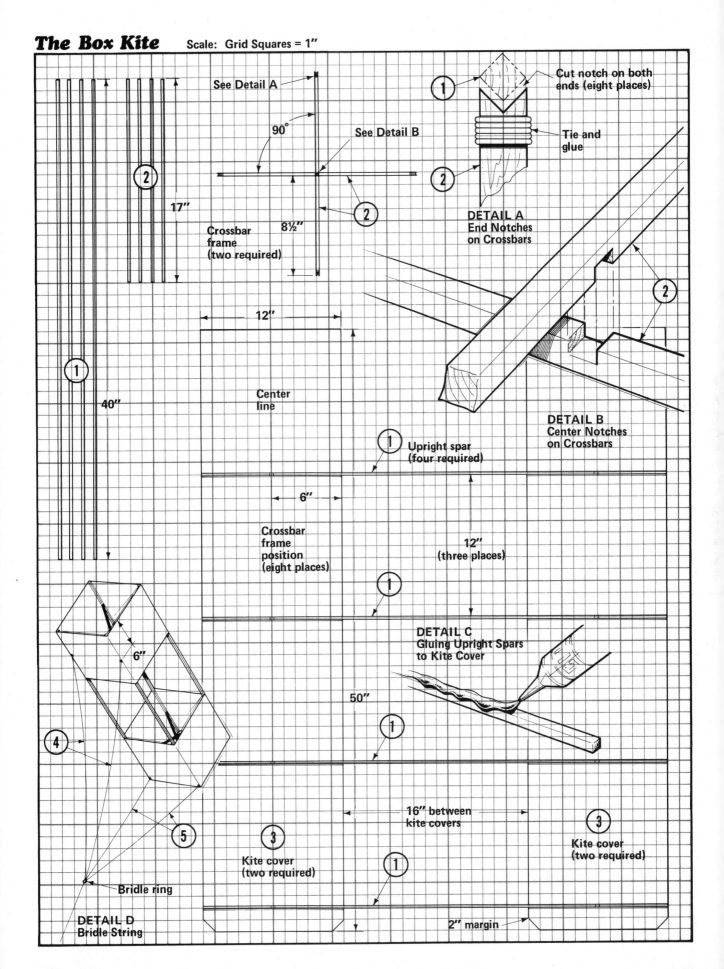

See Detail A

90°

See Detail B

17"

8½"

Crossbar
frame
(two required)

12"

Center
line

40"

6"

Crossbar
frame
position
(eight places)

Upright spar
(four required)

12"
(three places)

50"

6"

16" between
kite covers

Kite cover
(two required)

Kite cover
(two required)

Bridle ring

DETAIL D
Bridle String

2" margin

① Cut notch on both
ends (eight places)

② Tie and
glue

DETAIL A
End Notches
on Crossbars

DETAIL B
Center Notches
on Crossbars

DETAIL C
Gluing Upright Spars
to Kite Cover

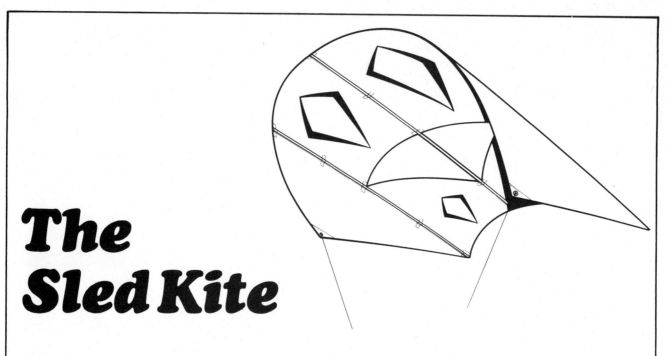

The Sled Kite

THE SLED KITE is a fairly recent entry in the sport of kite flying. Easily made, the sled kite consists simply of three spars to which a covering is attached with tape. It belongs to the general category known as flexible kites.

The sled kite flies best in light to moderate winds, and it can be quite difficult to launch and control in flight on gusty days. Because the sled kite has no lateral spars, it tends to fold up and collapse when hit by erratic or strong crosswinds. Unlike most of the other kites described in this book, the sled kite should be constructed in strict accordance with the directions given here; changing the specifications might very well result in your creating an unflyable kite.

Kite Frame Materials

FOR THE SLED kite, you will need three 36-inch spars [1] which will provide the stiffening elements in this flexible kite. Slender (quarter-inch thick) square-sectioned sticks of cypress, spruce, or pine or even birch dowels make good spars; bamboo is also suitable. All these materials are usually easy to obtain at most hobby shops and hardware stores.

How To Create A Sled Kite

THE FIRST STEP in creating a sled kite is to make the kite cover [2]. Start by making a paper pattern from which you will later cut the actual kite cover [2]. Draw a straight horizontal line 20 inches long on a piece of paper; then draw another horizontal line 20 inches long 36 inches directly below and parallel to the first line. Now, measure down from the left end of the top line and make a pencil mark at a point exactly ten inches below the top line and ten inches to the left of it.

Draw a straight line connecting the left end of the top line to the pencil mark, and then draw another straight line connecting the pencil mark to the left end of the lower line. To complete the outline for the sled kite pattern, make another pencil mark at a position that is ten inches below and ten inches to the right of the right end of the top line. Connect this pencil mark to the right end of the top line with a straight line, and then connect the pencil mark with the right end of the bottom line with another straight line.

The last step in drawing the sled kite pattern is to include a vent — the triangular-shaped hole in the kite cover [2]. First, make a pencil mark at a position that is 16 inches directly above the right end of the bottom line. Next, make another pencil mark at a position

Editor's Note: The numbers and detail citations that appear in brackets [ ] throughout this chapter refer to the scale drawing of The Sled Kite.

16 inches directly above the left end of the bottom line. Finally, make a mark six inches above the middle of the bottom line. When you draw a line connecting the three dots — use a straightedge or a ruler to be sure that all lines are absolutely straight — you will have a vent on your sled kite pattern.

Now cut out the paper pattern with sharp scissors or a razor blade. Be sure to cut out the vent in the lower middle section of the pattern. Fold the neatly cut pattern in half vertically down the center, and check to be sure that both halves are identical in size and do not overlap. Make any adjustment needed to create perfectly symmetrical halves.

For the sled kite, you will need a kite cover material like 200-gauge polyethylene, Tyvek, Mylar, or even lightweight cloth. The kite cover [2] can also be made from a large plastic trashbag. Paper, however, is not flexible enough to work well. If you select plastic, try dampening the underside so that it will lie flat as you cut it.

You are now ready to cut out the actual kite covering [2]. To insure a sharp and even cut, go around your paper pattern with a razor blade or very sharp scissors, cutting the covering [2] to the shape of a sled kite. Be sure to cut out the vent in the lower middle section of the kite covering [2]. Then fold the cover [2] in half just as you did with the paper pattern.

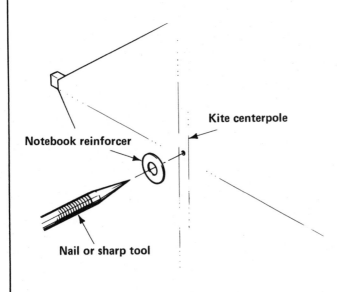

Kite centerpole

Notebook reinforcer

Nail or sharp tool

Punch holes in the kite cover for the bridle string.

Check to be sure that both sides are identical; if they are not, make any adjustments necessary.

Now spread out the kite cover [2] on a flat surface. Be sure that it lies absolutely flat, without any wrinkles, creases, or air bubbles. Position one of the 36-inch spars [1] so that it runs vertically from the left end of the top of the kite cover [2] to the left end of the bottom. Next, attach the spar [1] to the kite cover [2] with three-inch strips of tape [3] [Detail A]; waterproof adhesive tape or strapping tape work best. Secure the spar [1] to the kite cover [2] with tape [3] at nine-inch intervals, starting from the top.

Position the second spar [1] down the center of the kite cover [2]. Tape this spar [1] in position in the same manner as you secured the first spar, except that you must position the fourth piece of tape [3] 30 inches from the top instead of 27 inches to allow for the vent. Finally, position the last 36-inch spar [1] so that it runs vertically from the right end of the top to the right end of the bottom of the kite cover [2]. Tape it securely in place as you did the left-hand spar [1].

The final step in the creation of a sled kite is to prepare a two-legged bridle. Much of a sled kite's success in flight depends on its bridle. The bridle lines must be sufficiently long to allow the kite time to recover should strong crosswinds cause the kite to collapse.

Begin by inserting metal eyelets [4] or by making holes with a nail or sharp-pointed tool at the two outside corners of the kite. If you do not use eyelets [4] apply notebook reinforcers or tape around the holes to prevent tearing of the kite cover [2]. Next, cut a piece of bridle string [5] exactly 13 feet long. Carefully fold the bridle string [5] exactly in half, and make an overhand knot at its exact center. Now, measure 72 inches back on the bridle string [5] from the knot. Guide this end of the bridle string [5] through one of the holes in the kite cover [2] and tie the bridle string [5] securely to the kite at the 72-inch position. Guide the other end of the bridle string [5] through the other hole, and — measuring 72 inches from the knot — tie it securely to the kite.

You now have a sled kite that is ready to fly. If you find it difficult to keep the sled kite in flight, add a strip of cardboard across the top to form something akin to a crossbar. The true sled kite is fascinating to watch and an enjoyable challenge to fly.

The Sled Kite

Scale: Grid Squares = 1"

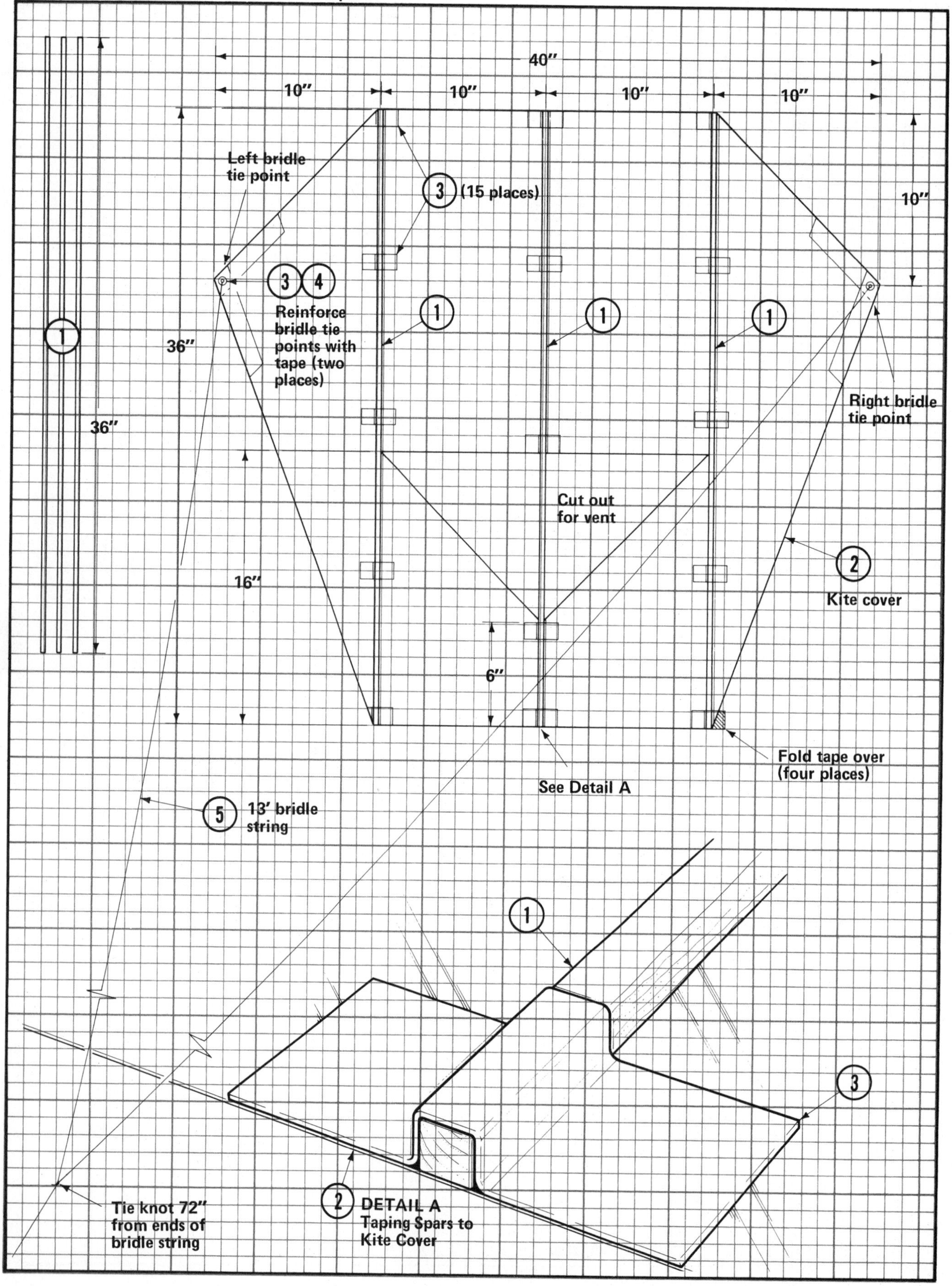

40"

10" 10" 10" 10"

10"

Left bridle
tie point

③ (15 places)

③ ④

Reinforce
bridle tie
points with
tape (two
places)

①

36"

36"

16"

6"

①

①

①

①

Right bridle
tie point

Cut out
for vent

②

Kite cover

Fold tape over
(four places)

See Detail A

⑤ 13' bridle
string

①

③

②

②

DETAIL A
Taping Spars to
Kite Cover

Tie knot 72"
from ends of
bridle string

The Tetrahedral Kite

WHEN HE WAS not busy inventing the telephone, Alexander Graham Bell found time to assemble the tetrahedral kite. His creation, a distinct refinement of the traditional box kite, was a new and exciting innovation in the category of cellular kites.

The word "tetrahedral" means four-sided, and the frame of a tetrahedral kite is simply a four-sided pyramid composed of equal triangular panels. Two sides of the pyramid frame are then covered to form the kite. Extremely strong and rigid by the nature of its pyramid frame, the tetrahedral kite has the advantage of not needing cross-bracing.

> **Editor's Note:** The numbers and detail citations that appear in brackets [ ] throughout this chapter refer to the scale drawing of The Tetrahedral Kite.

Cells, or tetrahedrons, can be joined together in just about any number to form kites of almost unlimited size. In fact, Alexander Graham Bell once joined 3393 cells together in what turned out to be a successful attempt to carry a human being aloft in a kite-craft.

The directions here are for a four-celled tetrahedral, which is much more effective in flight than a single-celled tetrahedral kite. The process of creating a multi-celled tetrahedral kite is really no different from building a single-celled kite; you simply lash the individual tetrahedral sections together. Keep in mind, however, that all lift surfaces must be facing the same direction.

These instructions provide measurements in terms of proportion because the cells of the tetrahedral kite can be constructed in a wide range of sizes.

Kite Frame Materials

YOU WILL NEED six spars of equal length for each cell. The type of material to use for the spars depends, of course, on the size of the kite you wish to make. A very small tetrahedral kite can be constructed from drinking straws, while very large kites require strong aluminum tubing for their frames. A good compromise for the kite described here would be slender, lightweight wooden spars; spruce, pine, whitewood dowels, or any other wood that combines both strength and lightness will suffice. You can obtain most of these woods easily at hobby stores, lumber shops, and hardware stores.

How To Create A Tetrahedral Kite

FOR THE four-celled tetrahedral kite, you will need 24 18-inch spars [1]. When you have them cut to the proper length, drill pilot holes and then insert screw eyes into both ends of all 24 spars [1] [Detail A]. Now lay three of the spars [1] on a table or flat surface to form a triangle. The next step is to lash the two screw eyes at each point of juncture with string [Detail B]. Use strong string that will not stretch and will not add bulk; a common four-ply cotton string is quite suitable. Lash the spars [1] in position by taking at least four turns through the screw eyes, and then tie with a square knot. Clip off any excess string.

Now take three more spars [1], and lash one end of each of these spars [1] to each of

the three corners or points of juncture of the existing triangle [Detail C]. Finally, join the remaining three ends of these spars by lashing with string to form a tetrahedron. Trim off any excess string, and then apply a liberal coating of glue to all knots; these knots must hold solidly and permanently. Any glue that dries quickly and becomes tough rather than brittle is appropriate for this job. Be sure that you use enough glue to soak the string of the joints and knots thoroughly, and then set this tetrahedral cell aside and allow it to dry. Now make three more tetrahedral cells in the same way that you constructed the first one.

Preparing The Kite Cover

WHEN THE FRAMES of all four cells are finished and the glue on each is completely dry, you are ready to prepare the kite covers [2] for each cell. Only two of the cell's four sides are to be covered with material. Select covering material that is lightweight but that is also quite strong. Mylar, plastic, polyethylene film, lightweight fabric, or strong paper (e.g., tissue paper, shelf paper, or wrapping paper) are suitable covering materials for a tetrahedral kite.

Fold the cover material in half, and place the frame of the cell on the covering with one side of the triangular base along the fold in the covering material. Now, take a pencil and trace around the outside edge of the other two sides of the triangle, leaving a half-inch margin on both sides. Later, you will overlap this margin around the frame and glue it. When you finish tracing the pattern, mark small rounded cutaways in the kite cover [2] at each point through which the corner spars [1] will protrude.

Once you have the pattern properly traced, you are ready to cut the kite covering [2] (still folded) to its correct shape. Use sharp scissors to get a clean cut, and then unfold the covering.

With the covering cut to size, it is time to decorate. Refer to the chapter "Decorating The Kite" and to the full-color illustration of The Tetrahedral Kite for ideas.

You are now ready to cover two adjacent sides of the tetrahedral cell [Detail D]. Carefully apply a thin line of glue to each spar [1] to which the kite covering [2] will be attached, and then place the covering [2] over the frame. Fold the overlap of the kite cover [2] around

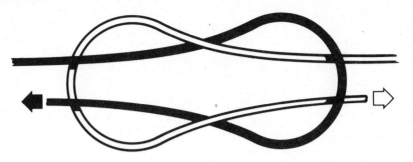

After lashing the spars that form the tetrahedral cell, tie the string ends into a square knot.

the spar [1] so that it will adhere firmly to the spar [1]. Work slowly in order to avoid wrinkles and creases as you seal the margin over the frame. Also be careful not to curve or bend the spars [1] out of shape. When you are finished, put that cell aside to dry, and repeat the same covering process with each of the other three tetrahedral cells.

When the glue is completely dry on all four cells, it is time to attach them to create a four-celled tetrahedral kite [Detail E]. Place two cells side by side, with the kite cover [2] on the bottom side and on the side facing you. Position a third tetrahedral cell behind these two cells, again with the kite cover [2] on the bottom and on the side facing you. Use string to lash the three points where these cells come together. Then place the fourth cell on top of the three cells at the three connecting points. Be sure that the lift surfaces, or kite covers [2], are facing in the same direction as that of the first three — kite cover on the bottom side and on the side facing you.

Now you must prepare a bridle; for the tetrahedral kite the bridle can either be a two-legged or four-legged version [Detail F]. To make a two-legged bridle, cut a length of bridle string [3] approximately six times as long as one of the spars [1]. Tie one end of the bridle string securely to the frame of the lower cell on the right-hand side when facing you. Guide the other end of the bridle string two or three times through a bridle ring (a curtain ring will suffice for this purpose) and then attach this end of the string to the frame of the lower left cell.

If you prefer a four-legged bridle, cut another piece of bridle string [4] 1½ times the length of the first bridle string [3]. Attach it to the frame of the cell at your upper right. Guide the other end of the bridle string [4] two or three times through the bridle ring, and then tie the end of the bridle string [4] securely to the frame of the cell at your upper left.

The four-celled tetrahedral kite is now complete. It will fly best in a moderate to heavy wind, and it should display an excellent degree of self-correction because of its dihedral angle.

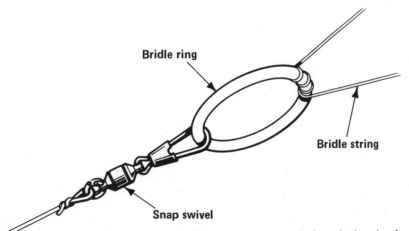

A swivel attachment connecting the flying line and the bridle ring is a great help in reducing the frequency of tangled lines.

The Tetrahedral Kite   Scale: Grid Squares = 1"

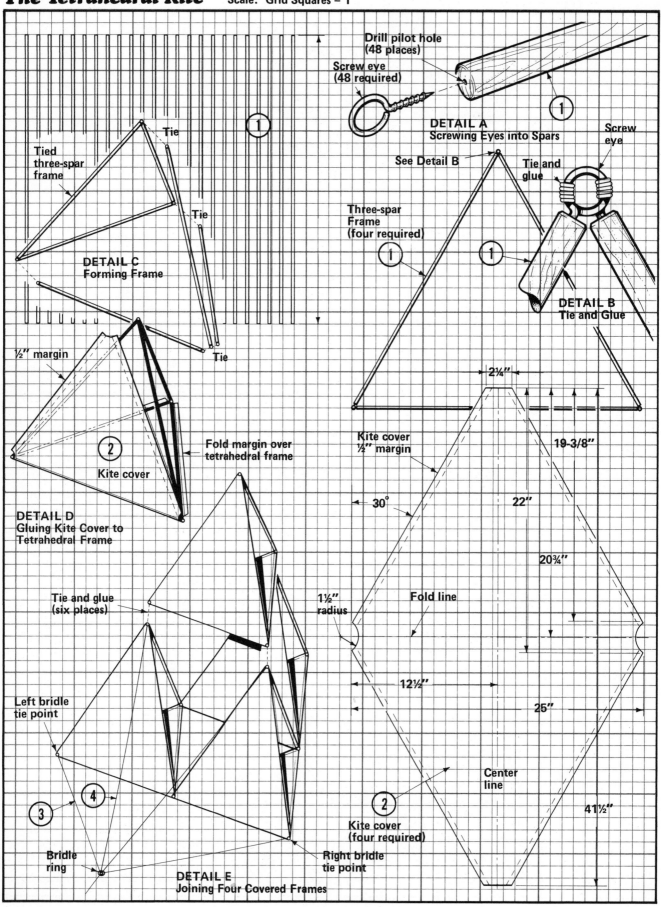

Drill pilot hole
(48 places)

Screw eye
(48 required)

DETAIL A
Screwing Eyes into Spars

Tie

Tied
three-spar
frame

Tie

Tie

DETAIL C
Forming Frame

Tie

See Detail B

Tie and
glue

Three-spar
Frame
(four required)

Screw
eye

DETAIL B
Tie and Glue

½" margin

Fold margin over
tetrahedral frame

Kite cover

DETAIL D
Gluing Kite Cover to
Tetrahedral Frame

2¼"

Kite cover
½" margin

19-3/8"

30°

22"

20¾"

Tie and glue
(six places)

Fold line

1½"
radius

Left bridle
tie point

12½"

25"

Bridle
ring

Center
line

41½"

Right bridle
tie point

DETAIL E
Joining Four Covered Frames

Kite cover
(four required)

The Star Kite

THE STAR-SHAPED kite is a traditional Chinese design. For centuries this five-, six-, or eight-pointed kite has been a special favorite with children and a popular kite with adults as well. Striking even with a simple, plain covering, the star kite can, of course, be elaborately decorated. It flies well in moderate winds, and the overall effect — with the star kite's many paper streamer tails fluttering in the breeze — can be quite spectacular.

Kite Frame Materials

YOU WILL NEED four spars of equal length to construct the frame of the star kite. Split bamboo is an ideal frame material because it is both strong and lightweight; but if bamboo is unavailable, you can fashion the spars of square-sectioned hardwood or softwood (spruce or cypress), which you can buy at almost any hobby shop or lumber mart.

How To Create A Star Kite

BEGIN BY cutting the four spars [1] to exactly

equal lengths. The measurements that follow can be modified somewhat as long as they are kept in proportion; the size of your kite can suit your particular wishes, but each spar [1]

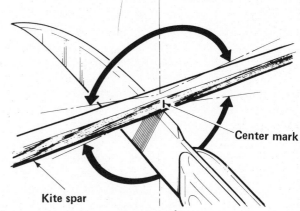

Center mark

Kite spar

Balance each spar on a knife blade's edge.

Editor's Note: The numbers and detail citations that appear in brackets [ ] throughout this chapter refer to the scale drawing of The Star Kite.

should be at least 24 inches in length to provide a kite that will fly at maximum efficiency.

Once you cut the spars [1] to size, you must test each one for balance. Draw a pencil line across the exact center of each spar [1], and then balance the spar [1] at this point on the edge of a knife blade. If the spar [1] fails to rest on a relatively horizontal plane, you must correct the imbalance before proceeding. Pare down the heavier side of the spar [1] with sandpaper or a knife until it balances properly.

When all the spars [1] balance, use a sharp knife or saw to cut a notch in both ends of each one. Later, these notches will hold the guide string. Since notching can cause the bamboo or wood to split or crack when a great deal of pressure is applied, however, be sure to lash the spar [1] with ordinary string just below the notch. The string will reinforce the wood and prevent it from splitting or cracking under the strain.

Now set two of the spars [1] aside, and position the remaining two spars [1] so that they form an "X." These two spars [1] must intersect at the center mark on each, and their ends must be an equal distance apart. Next, cut an eight-inch length of common four-ply cotton string or any other strong, inelastic, and non-bulking string. Lash the two spars [1] in position by taking at least two turns through both diagonals at their crossing point. Then weave the string over and under the sticks, and tie it with a square knot. Cut off any extra string that remains after knotting.

Test the balance of this "X" frame you just created. It is most important that the frame balance on either side of its point of juncture. Place one end of one spar [1] on a table and rest the other end of the same spar [1] on the tip of your finger. The frame should rest along a horizontal plane. After testing one spar's [1] balance, repeat the same procedure to test the balance of the other spar [1].

If the frame tends to dip to one side, correct any imbalance before proceeding. To correct a frame imbalance, first check to be sure that the two spars [1] are joined at their exact centers. If not, adjust the lashing until the spars [1] are perfectly centered. Next, check to see if one side of the frame is heavier than the other. If this is the case, whittle or sandpaper the heavier side until the frame balances as it should.

Now take the two remaining spars [1] and

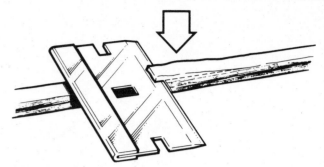

Pare the spar's heavier side until it balances.

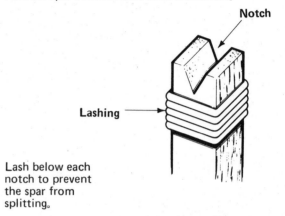

Lash below each notch to prevent the spar from splitting.

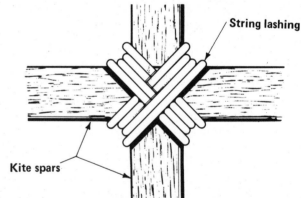

Lash the spars together by wrapping their point of juncture with string.

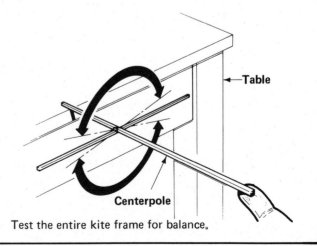

Test the entire kite frame for balance.

create another "X" frame. Lash the spars [1] together and test the frame for balance just as you did with the first "X" frame.

When you are satisfied that both frames balance, coat the string lashings of both thoroughly with glue. Any quick-drying glue that will not become brittle is appropriate for this job. Be sure that you use enough glue to soak the entire area of the joints and knots. Now set the frames aside and allow them to dry.

When the glue on the two frames dries completely, it is time to fasten a string guideline [2] to each. The purpose of the string guideline [2] is to create a firm edge for mounting the kite cover. Use the same strong string you used to lash the joints of the "X" frames.

Take the first "X" frame and attach the string guideline [2] to the notch at one end of one spar [1]; secure it tightly with a square knot. Run the string guideline [2] to the notch in the next spar [1], and attach it to this spar [1] in the same manner. Continue the string guideline [2] on around the frame, keeping it taut at all times until you get back to where you started. Then tie the two ends of the string guideline [2] together to form a taut, secure guideline around the frame. Now repeat the same process with the second "X" frame.

At this point, you are ready to join the two "X" frames together. Place the first "X" frame on a flat surface, and place the second "X" frame on top of it so that the spars [1] of the second frame are positioned midway between the spars [1] of the first frame. Now lash the two "X" frames together securely; take the string through each diagonal of the crossing point. Next, test the balance of the combined frame as you tested each of the frames separately. Then soak the point of juncture with glue and allow the frame to dry.

Preparing The Kite Cover

YOU ARE NOW ready to prepare the kite's cover [3]. The star kite can be covered with either paper or a lightweight fabric but the covering material selected must be strong and non-porous so that the wind cannot blow through it. Suitable papers include anything from wrapping paper to tissue paper, newspaper, shelf paper, brown paper, rice paper, or the imitation Japanese paper found in art supply stores. Suitable synthetics or fabrics in-

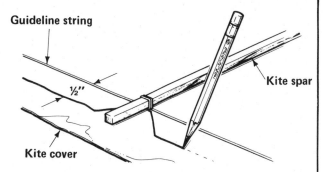

Trace around the outside edge of the frame, leaving a half-inch margin all around.

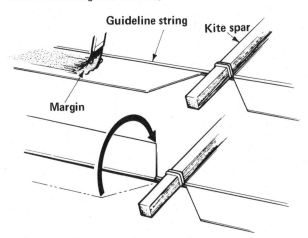

Apply glue to the margin and seal it securely with the string guideline inside.

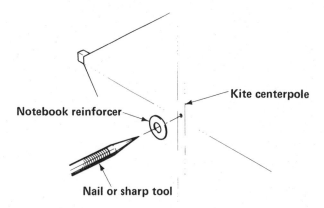

Punch four holes in the kite cover where the bridle will be attached.

clude most of the polyethylene materials available in kite stores or art and stationery shops.

Place the kite frame on the kite cover [3], and trace around the outside edge of the frame with a pencil, leaving a half-inch margin all around. Later, you will glue this margin to overlap the string guideline [2]. But first mark a notch where each spar [1] will protrude, and then cut out the pattern from the material, using sharp scissors for a straight and clean edge.

With the kite cover [3] cut to size, notch the hem at each of the eight points of the star. The notches facilitate folding the kite cover [3] over the string guideline [2].

This would be a good point to stop construction and start decorating the kite. You can get some ideas and learn some techniques for this important aspect of kite-creating by studying both the chapter "Decorating The Kite" and the full-color illustration of the Star Kite.

When you finish the kite decoration — all paints, glues, or other fluid items are totally dry — you can mount the kite cover [3] on the frame. Position the frame over the covering [3], and crease the margin over the string guideline [2]. Apply glue to the margin, and seal it securely with the string guideline [2] inside. Work carefully to avoid wrinkles and creases. If you selected a fabric covering, you have your choice either to glue or sew it (with a running stitch) to the string guideline [2].

The next step is to prepare a four-legged bridle, which is necessary to control the angle at which the surface of the star kite meets the wind. You must make four holes in the kite covering [3] at the four points where the bridle will be attached. Use a nail or a pointed tool to punch a hole in the covering [3] about two inches from the bottom of and directly over the middle spar [1], which is serving here as a centerpole. Place a notebook reinforcer around the hole to prevent the kite cover [3] from tearing. Now carefully punch another hole six inches from the top of the centerpole, and add a notebook reinforcer to this hole, too. Punch the last two holes over the two spars [1] adjacent to the centerpole, six inches from their top ends, and apply notebook reinforcers to these holes.

Now, cut a piece of bridle string [4] twice the length of one of the spars [1]. Guide one end of the bridle string [4] through the hole above the spar [1] that is to your left of the centerpole, and tie that end securely to the frame. Now loop the bridle string [4] two or three times through the bridle ring; a curtain ring makes a good bridle ring.

Slide the bridle ring along the bridle string [4] until it is approximately halfway up the length of the bridle string [4]. Now guide the loose end of the bridle string [4] through the hole above the spar [1] to the right of the centerpole, and tie it securely to the frame.

Cut another piece of bridle string [5] that measures 2¼ times the length of a spar [1]. Take one end of this bridle string [5] through the hole toward the upper end of the centerpole and tie it to the frame. Then loop it two or three times through the bridle ring at the point where the distance from the end tied to the centerpole to the bridle ring is exactly equal to the distance to the bridle ring of each of the other two tied ends of the bridle string [4]. Then guide the other end of the string [5] through the hole at the bottom of the centerpole, and tie it securely to the frame. The length of bridle string [5] from the bridle ring to this hole will be longer than the other three. When you finish lashing the bridle strings [4 and 5], do not trim any of the excess string from the knots; you may need it later for flight adjustments.

The final step in the creation of a star kite is the preparation of the tail. All flat kites must have a tail for flight stability. A star kite tail is usually made of crepe paper or tissue paper streamers, although it can be made of lightweight cloth. To make a tail [6] consisting of three paper streamers, you would glue one streamer to the lower end of the centerpole and the other two on either side at 90-degree angles to the first tail [6]. In a three-streamer tail [6], each streamer should be five times the length of a spar [1].

For a really spectacular sight, attach a five-streamer tail, in which one streamer is glued to each of the five bottom points of the star. In a five-streamer tail, the bottom streamer is the longest — three times the length of a spar [1]. The two other bottommost streamers on either side of the long streamer should each be twice as long as a spar [1]. The remaining two streamers should each equal the length of one spar [1].

You may need to adjust the tail so that it provides stability by its weight as well as by its air resistance. Varying wind conditions may dictate changes during flight-testing. If the kite tends to loop and spin, lengthen the tail. If the tail seems to restrict the kite's movement, shorten it. You can also affect the kite's wind resistance by fringing the paper streamers or by adding tassels.

The Star Kite

Scale: Grid Squares = ½"

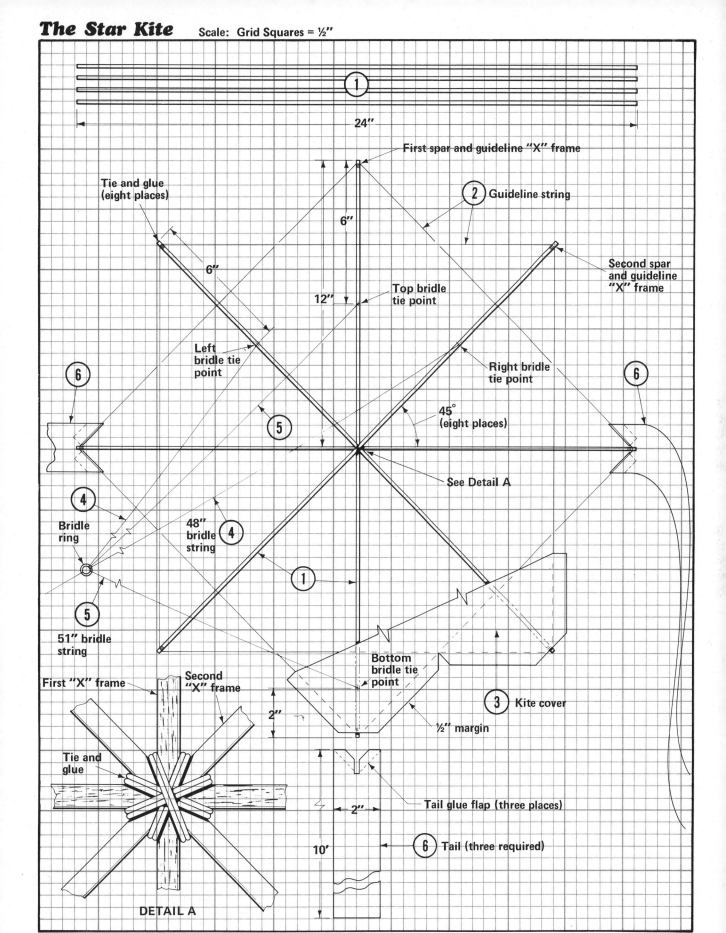

First spar and guideline "X" frame

① ② Guideline string

6"

6"

Tie and glue (eight places)

Second spar and guideline "X" frame

Top bridle tie point

12"

Left bridle tie point

Right bridle tie point

⑥ ⑥

45° (eight places)

⑤

See Detail A

④ ④ 48" bridle string

Bridle ring

① ⑤

51" bridle string

Bottom bridle tie point

③ Kite cover

First "X" frame

Second "X" frame

2"

½" margin

Tie and glue

Tail glue flap (three places)

2"

10'

⑥ Tail (three required)

DETAIL A

The Rectangular Kite

THE EARLIEST kites in China, those made several thousand years ago, probably resembled the flat rectangular kite described here. The Chinese decorated their rectangular kites ornately, with elaborate paintings of warriors, battles, and other dramatic scenes. Today, the rectangular kite is still very popular in most areas of Asia, particularly so in Japan.

The flat rectangular kite is an easy one to construct, and it flies exceptionally well in light to gentle winds. It can be built to practically any size — large or small — but the most flyable version measures approximately 48 inches by 32 inches.

Kite Frame Materials

SPLIT BAMBOO is the most effective material for constructing the frame of a rectangular kite; it is both strong and lightweight. You can often find the split bamboo you need for kite frames in discarded outdoor porch shades, but if bamboo is unavailable, you can fashion the spars from square-sectioned sticks of spruce or cypress which are readily available at hobby shops and lumber stores.

You will need four spars to construct the frame of the rectangular kite. The longest spar forms the centerpole [1]. The three shorter spars — which are all equal in length — form the crossbars [2], which are two-thirds the length of the centerpole [1].

Editor's Note: The numbers and detail citations that appear in brackets [ ] throughout this chapter refer to the scale drawing of The Rectangular Kite.

How To Create A Rectangular Kite

WHEN YOU FINISH cutting the centerpole [1] and crossbars [2] to their appropriate lengths, you must test them for balance. Mark each one at the exact center of its length, and then balance each on the edge of a knife at this center mark. If the centerpole [1] or any of the crossbars fails to hover on a relatively horizontal plane, you must correct the imbalance by paring down the heavier side with sandpaper or a knife until it balances properly.

The next step is to cut notches in both ends of the three crossbars [2]. Later, these notches will hold the guideline string [3]. Since notching can weaken a spar and lead to splitting or cracking when pressure is applied, you should lash each end of the crossbar [2] with string just below the notch.

You are now ready to lash the centerpole [1] and crossbars [2] together. Start by placing the centerpole [1] on a flat surface. Now lay one of the crossbars [2] perpendicular to the centerpole [1] one inch down from the top of the centerpole [1]. Make sure that the center mark on this crossbar [2] rests directly over the centerpole [1].

Lash the point of juncture with strong, inelastic, and non-bulking string; common four-ply cotton string will suffice. The best way to lash the centerpole [1] and crossbar [2] in position is to run the string at least two turns through both diagonals of the crossing point, weaving it over and under and then tying the ends with a square knot. After the knot is secure, clip off any excess string.

Now position the second crossbar [2] perpendicular to the centerpole [1], with its center mark directly over and 20 inches down from the top of the centerpole [1]. Lash it to the centerpole [1] in the same manner you did the first crossbar [2].

Position the third crossbar [2] similarly, with its center mark directly over and five inches up from the bottom of the centerpole [1]. Lash it securely to the centerpole [1].

At this point, you must test the balance of the entire kite frame. It is of crucial importance that the frame balance perfectly on either side of the centerpole [1]. In order to test for balance, place the top end of the centerpole [1] on a table and rest the other end on the tip of your finger. The entire frame should lay along a horizontal plane. If the frame tends to dip to one side, it is not balanced, and you must cor-

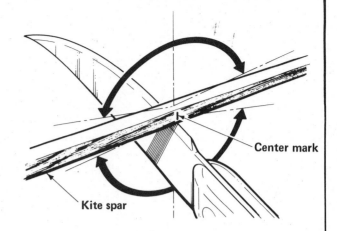

Balance each spar on a knife blade's edge.

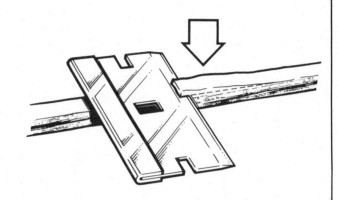

Trim the spar's heavier side so that it balances.

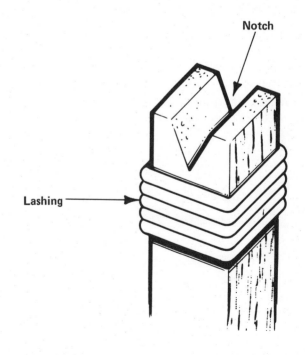

Lash below each notch to prevent the spar from splitting.

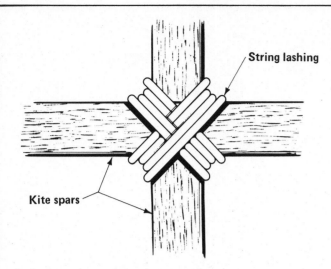

Lash the center and crossbars together.

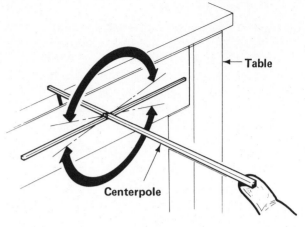

Test the balance of the entire kite frame.

rect the imbalance before proceeding. First check your measurements to be sure that the centerpole crosses the exact center of each crossbar; if it does not, adjust the lashing until it does. Next, if the frame still fails to balance properly, whittle or sandpaper the heavier side of the crossbar [2] (or crossbars [2]) until the frame is evenly weighted on either side of the centerpole [1].

When the frame balances properly, apply glue to all the lashings. Any glue that dries quickly and does not become brittle is appropriate for this job. Just be sure to use enough glue to soak the string of the joints and knots thoroughly. When the glue is dry, you have completed construction of the rectangular kite frame.

The next step is to lash the crossbars [2] with a string guideline [3]. The string guideline

[3] will make a firm rim around the frame on which to mount the kite cover [4] as well as maintain the kite's shape during flight. Use the same strong string for the guideline [3] that you used earlier to lash the joints.

Tie the string guideline [3] to the notch in the top crossbar [2], and then continue it on to the middle crossbar [2] where you guide it through the notch, pull it as taut as possible, and loop it securely around the crossbar [2]. Finally, run the string guideline [3] down to the bottom crossbar [2], keeping the string taut as you guide it through the notch and tie it securely. Repeat this process on the other side of the frame.

Preparing The Kite Cover

YOU ARE NOW ready to prepare the kite cover. Any resilient, strong, lightweight, non-porous paper such as newspaper, shelf paper, brown paper, wrapping paper, rice paper, or imitation Japanese paper (available in art supply stores) is quite suitable for use in covering the rectangular kite.

Place the kite frame on top of the kite cover [4], and trace with a pencil around the outside edge of the frame (the string guideline [3]), leaving a half-inch margin on all sides except the side along the bottom of the kite; provide a two-inch margin along this bottom side. Since the kite cover [4] will be slightly larger than the kite frame, make additional markings at each point where the crossbars [2] will protrude.

After lashing, tie the string ends into a square knot.

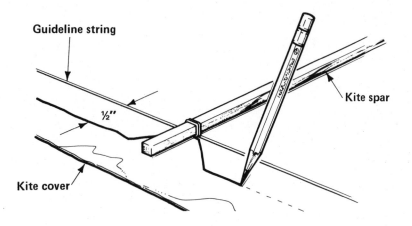

Trace around the string guideline, leaving a half-inch margin on all sides except the side along the bottom of the kite. Leave a two-inch margin along this bottom side.

Once the kite pattern is properly traced on the kite cover, cut it out. Use sharp scissors to maintain a clean, crisp cut.

At this point, with the kite covering [4] cut to size, it is time to decorate. Decoration of the rectangular kite can be as simple or as elaborate as you desire. You will find ideas as well as hints, precautions, and techniques in the chapter "Decorating the Kite," and you should also take a close look at the full-color illustration of The Rectangular Kite. If you decorate with paint, make sure it is completely dry before proceeding any further in assembling this kite.

Now position the kite frame over the undecorated side of the kite cover [4], with the crossbars [2] against the covering [4] and the centerpole [1] above it. Crease the half-inch margin over the crossbar [2] at the top and the string guideline [3] along both sides. Then apply glue to the margin surrounding these three sides, and seal the margin securely with the crossbar [2] and string guideline [3] inside. Glue the margin smoothly, avoiding any wrinkles or creases. You leave the bottom margin loose to form a flap that will provide a stabilizing drag for the rectangular kite when it is airborne.

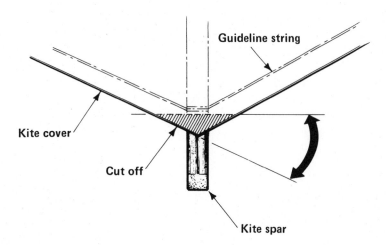

Since the kite cover will be slightly larger than the kite frame, make additional markings at each point where the crossbars will protrude.

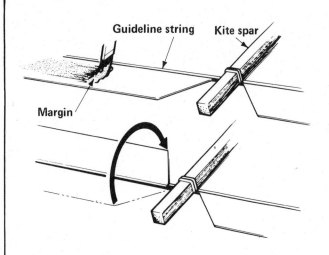

Guideline string   Kite spar

Margin

Apply glue to the margin and seal it with the crossbar and string guideline inside.

The rectangular kite requires a three-legged bridle to control the angle at which the surface of the kite meets the wind. With a nail or sharp-pointed tool, carefully punch a hole in the kite cover [4] directly over the joint formed by the centerpole [1] and the middle crossbar [2]. Place a notebook reinforcer around the hole to prevent tearing. Punch another hole in the covering [4] directly over the joint formed by the centerpole [1] and the bottom crossbar [2], and apply another notebook reinforcer to this hole. Then measure the distance from the top of the centerpole [1] to the hole above the

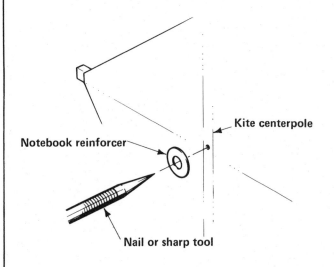

Kite centerpole

Notebook reinforcer

Nail or sharp tool

Punch holes in the kite cover for the bridle string.

bottom crossbar [2]. If you followed the measurements given here, the distance should be 42 inches. Cut one length of bridle string [5] four times this measurement — 168 inches — and another piece of bridle string [6] twice the measurement, or 84 inches in this case.

Now take the longer piece of bridle string [5] and tie one end securely to the top of the centerpole [1] just above the top crossbar [2]. Guide the other end of the bridle string [5] through a bridle ring — a curtain ring will serve this purpose — and loop the bridle string [5] through the ring. Finally, run the end of the string through the hole you punched in the bottom of the cover, and tie it securely to the frame.

You can adjust the placement of the bridle ring by sliding it along the bridle string [5]; position it approximately at the halfway mark of the bridle string [5] (which will put it nearer the top of the kite). Now take the shorter bridle string [6] and tie one end to the bridle ring. Run the other end through the hole at the center of the kite, and tie it to the frame. It may be necessary to adjust the position of the bridle ring further at this point in order to center it, but once you get it situated properly you should wrap a small piece of adhesive tape around the bridle ring to hold the bridle strings [5 and 6] secure.

The final step in creating a rectangular kite consists of preparing the tail [7]. One long paper streamer [7] glued to the bottom of the centerpole [1] should be adequate, although you can make a more elaborate tail by gluing several crepe paper or tissue paper streamers on either side at the bottom of the kite cover [4]. Do not, however, attach intersecting strips on the streamers of a double tail because they tend to tangle.

The tail [7] must provide stability for the kite by its weight and by its air resistance. You can fringe the paper streamers [7] to accommodate air resistance. If the kite tends to loop and spin, though, you must lengthen the tail [7]. On the other hand, if the tail [7] seems to restrict the kite's movement, shorten it. You must, in other words, match the tail [7] to the prevailing wind conditions.

This is one of the more basic rectangular kites. You can make much larger and/or much more complex versions. In the larger rectangular kites, you replace the string guideline [3] with additional spars in order to form a solid, heavy-duty frame.

The Rectangular Kite   Scale: Grid Squares = 1"

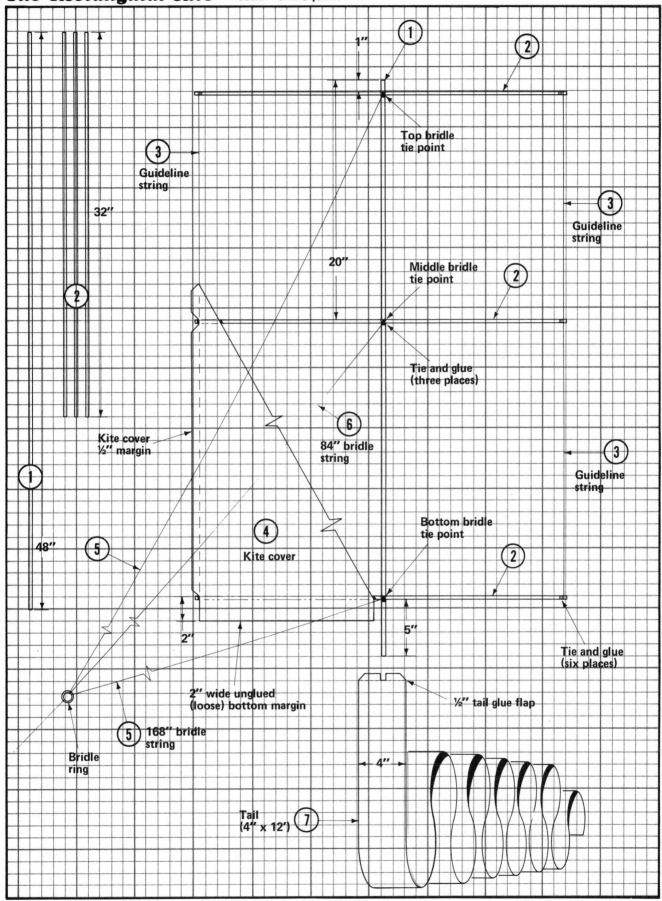

Top bridle tie point

Guideline string

32"

20"

Middle bridle tie point

Tie and glue (three places)

Kite cover ½" margin

84" bridle string

Guideline string

Guideline string

Kite cover

Bottom bridle tie point

48"

5"

Tie and glue (six places)

2"

2" wide unglued (loose) bottom margin

½" tail glue flap

168" bridle string

Bridle ring

4"

Tail (4" x 12')

The Kite of Circles

THE KITE OF CIRCLES is one of the less complicated paneled kites, but it provides a unique and fascinating sight in the sky. Sometimes called the Chinese orange kite because in China it was often decorated to appear as a cluster of oranges, the kite of circles provides a broad range for interesting and imaginative decoration.

The basic frame of this kite — the centerpole and crossbar — is similar in shape to the familiar diamond kite. But to the basic frame the kite creator adds four individually constructed circles (or panels) lashed together.

Kite Frame Materials

MAKE THE BASIC frame and the frames of the circular panels from bamboo. Not only is bamboo lightweight and strong, but more importantly it has the flexibility to be formed into circles. You can purchase split bamboo at many craft or hobby stores, but discarded outdoor porch shades are an excellent source of split bamboo. It is also possible to split your own bamboo from an old cane or pole.

To construct the frame of the kite of circles, you will need six square-sectioned quarter-inch spars. Four spars [1] of equal length will form the four circles.

How To Create A Kite Of Circles

THE DIRECTIONS here are given in proportions as well as in inches because the kite of circles can be constructed in several different sizes. For a fairly large kite — like the one described here — the circumference of each

---

Editor's Note: The numbers and detail citations that appear in brackets [ ] throughout this chapter refer to the scale drawing of The Kite of Circles.

The Malay Kite

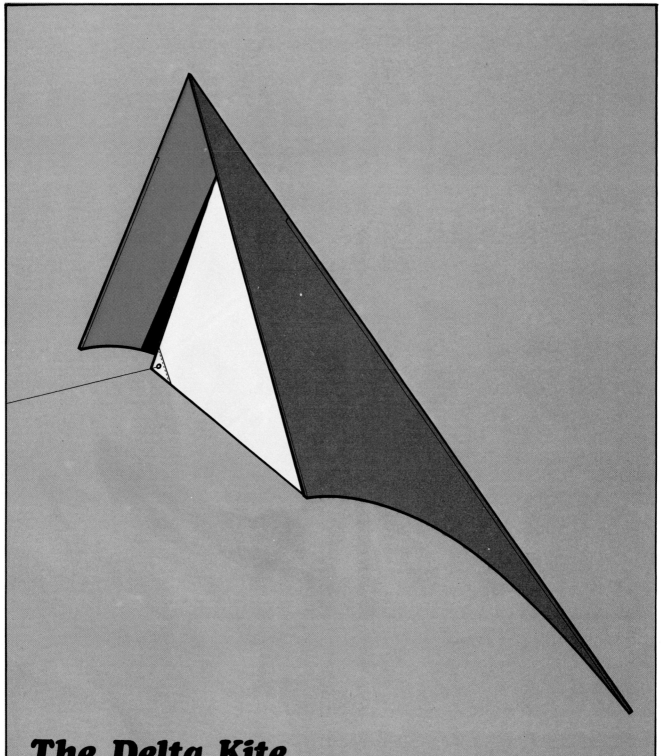

The Delta Kite

The Sled Kite

The Tetrahedral Kite

The Box Kite

The Rectangular Kite

The Star Kite

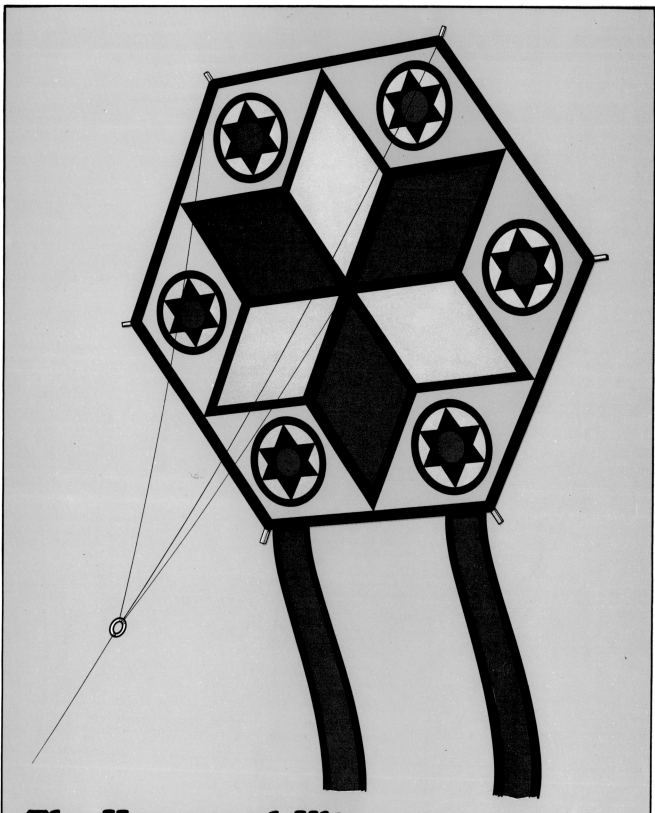

The Hexagonal Kite

The Bird Kite

The Kite of Circles

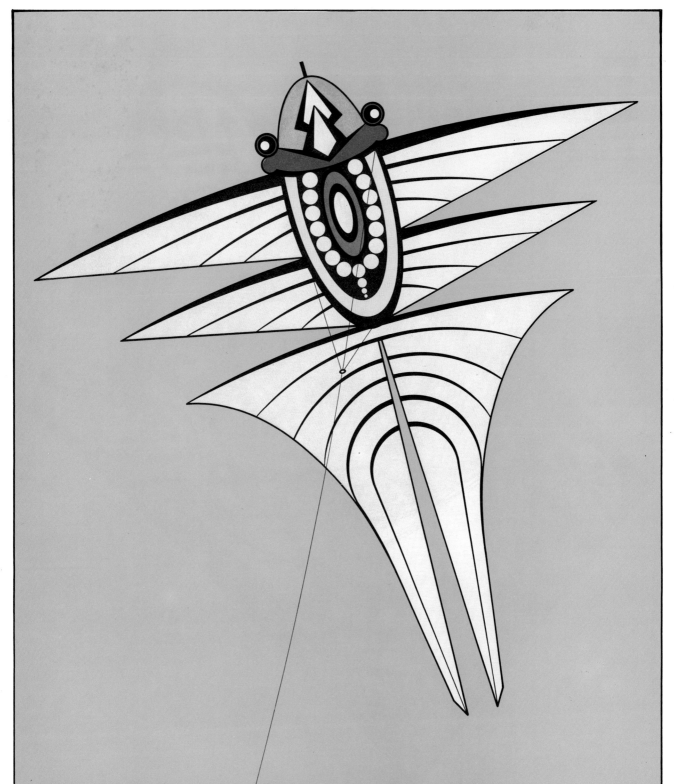

The Chinese Dragonfly Kite

The Asian Fighting Kite

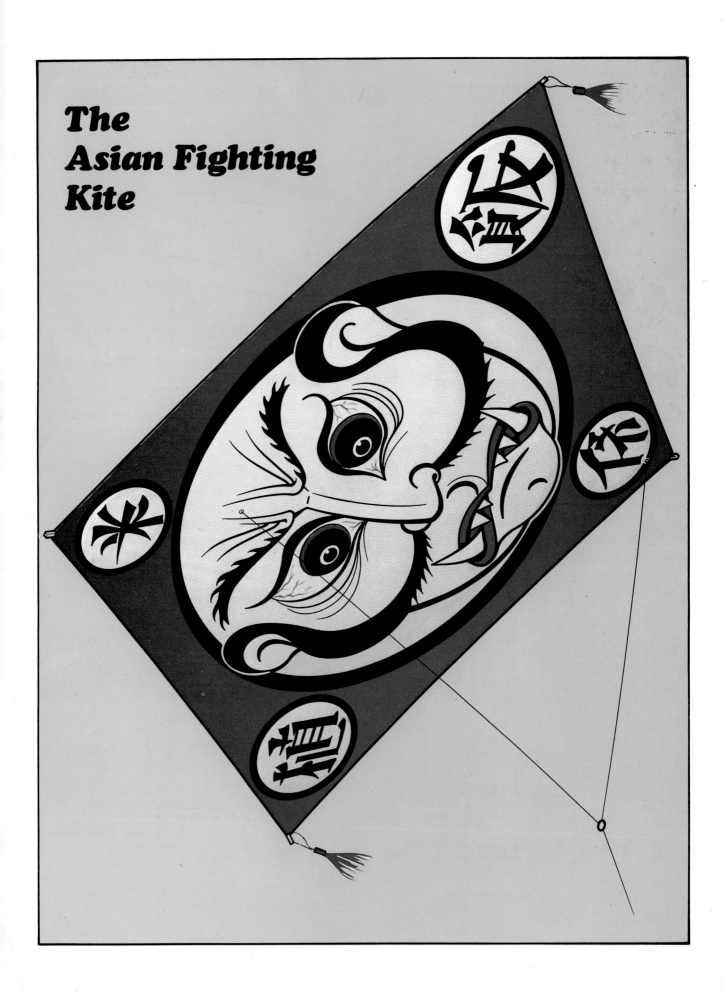

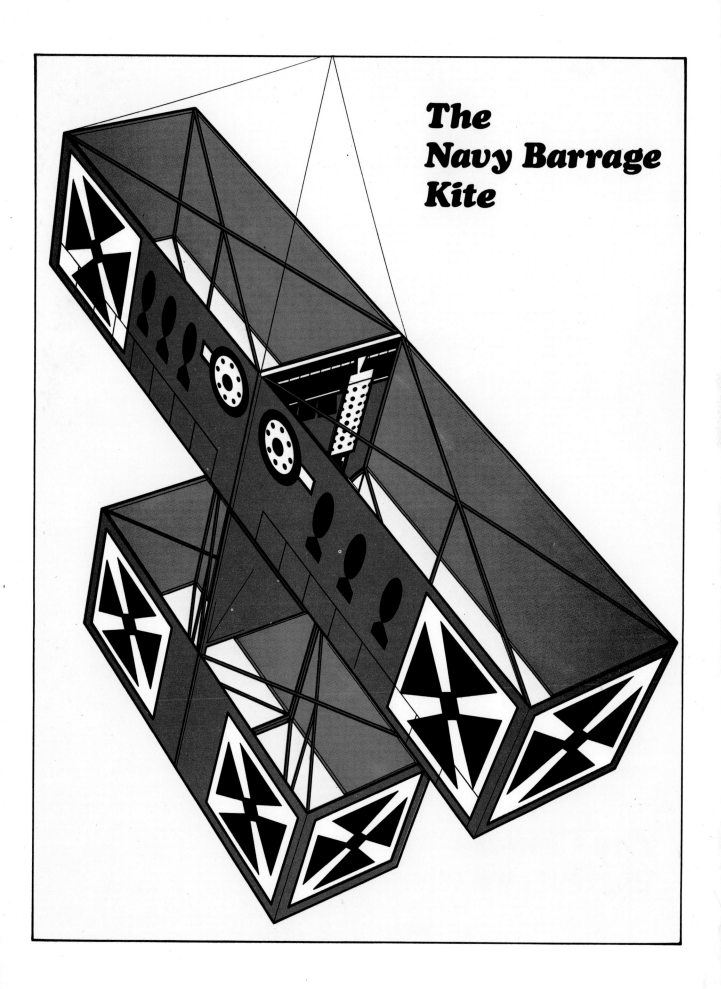

The
Navy Barrage
Kite

The Chinese
Butterfly Kite

The Elaborate
Parafoil Kite

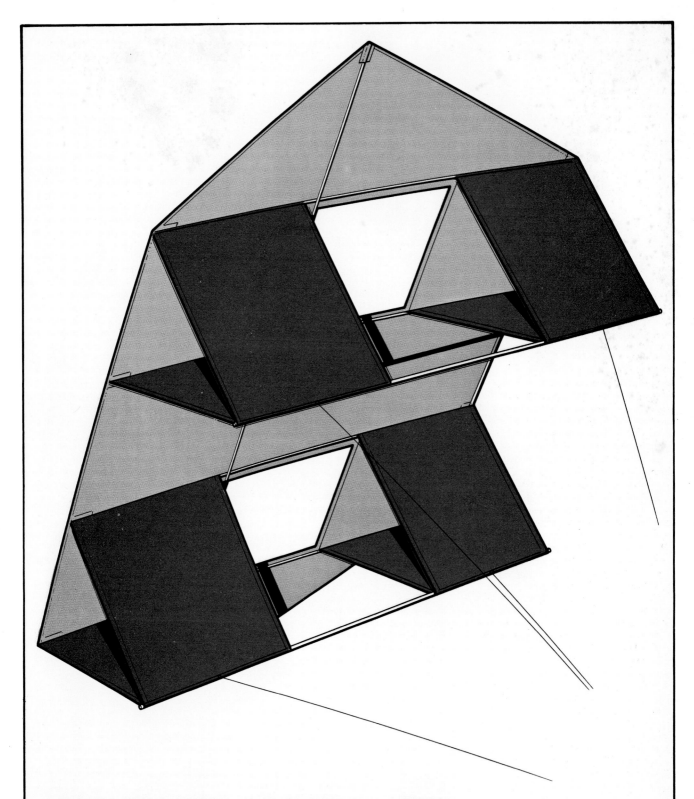

The Double Conyne Kite

circle might be 36 inches.

You must prepare the spars [1], of course, before you can bend them into circles. First check to be sure that the spars [1] bend evenly along their full length and that they are relatively free of irregularities like bumps or ridges. The bamboo must be able to retain a circular shape after it is formed, and it must be free of irregularities which might affect its balance.

The bamboo can be prepared for shaping in either of two ways. You can soak the four bamboo spars [1] in water for approximately two hours so that they will bend without breaking. A much quicker shaping method, however, is to move the bamboo spar [1] back and forth above a candle flame while applying pressure in the direction you want it to bend. Be careful, though, not to hold the bamboo motionless over the flame because it could burn or become permanently deformed and, therefore, lose its value as a framing spar.

When the bamboo is satisfactorily flexible, you are ready to form the circles. You will find it helpful to have a piece of paper on which you have drawn a perfect circle of the correct size to use as a shaping guide for the circular spars [1].

Begin by notching each end of the circular spars [1] to facilitate lashing [Detail A]. Now overlap the notched ends approximately a half-inch to form the desired circle, and glue the joint binding the circle. Use any glue that dries quickly and does not become brittle. Next, lash the joint with strong, inelastic, and non-bulky string; when joining two surfaces that run parallel, it is best to make two lashings as far apart as possible on the joint. Make a square knot or tie the knot twice on each lashing. After you complete the lashing process, soak all the string thoroughly with glue and allow it to dry.

With the frames of the four circles finished, you are ready to construct the kite's basic frame. First measure the diameter of one circular spar [1] frame. The crossbar [2] must be 2.2 times this measurement — or, in this case, 25 inches long. The centerpole [3] must be four times the diameter measurement or 44 inches long in the kite composed of 36-inch circular spars [1].

Cut the crossbar [2] and centerpole [3] to their proper lengths, and then measure and mark each one at the exact center of its length.

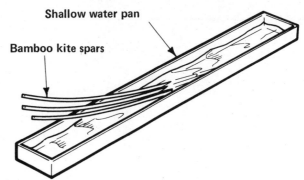

Soak the spars in water for two hours to make them flexible.

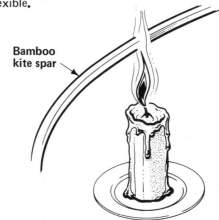

Move the spar back and forth over a candle flame while bending it.

Shave off bumps or irregularities from the spars before shaping them into circles.

Now place the centerpole [3] on a flat surface and position the crossbar [2] on the centerpole [3]. To determine precisely where the crossbar should be placed, measure down from the top of the centerpole [3] and position the crossbar at a point that is 1¾ times — 19¼ inches in the present case — the diameter of a circular spar [1] frame. Be sure also that the crossbar's [2] center mark is directly over the centerpole [3].

Now, with the crossbar [2] and centerpole [3] in position, lash the joint with string. Be sure to take at least two turns through both

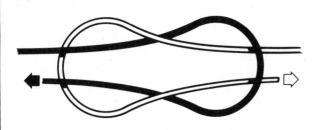

After lashing the circular spars, tie the string ends in a square knot.

diagonals of the crossing point, and then weave the string over and under. Tie the string with a square knot and clip off any excess.

You are now ready to attach the four circular spar [1] frames to the basic kite frame. Position two of the circular spar [1] frames so that one is on either side of the centerpole [3] and that each is centered over the crossbar [2]. Lash the circular spar [1] frames securely to both the crossbar [2] and centerpole [3]. Since you are again tying two surfaces that run parallel, you must be sure to lash the joint in two places.

Now position one of the remaining circular spar [1] frames so that it is centered directly over the centerpole [3] just above and touching the two previously positioned circular spar [1] frames. Lash this circular spar [1] frame securely to the centerpole [3] at its top and bottom, being sure to take the string twice through both diagonals.

Place the last circular spar [1] frame so that it is centered over the centerpole [3] at a position just below the first two circular spar [1] frames. Lash this last circular spar [1] frame securely to the centerpole [3] at the two places that it crosses the centerpole [3], again taking the string through both diagonals of the joint.

Finally, make parallel lashings at each of the four points where the circular spar [1] frames touch each other.

At this point, you must test the balance of the frame. Place one end of the centerpole [3] on a table, and rest the other end on the tip of your finger. The frame should remain in a horizontal plane. If the frame tends to dip to one side, however, you must correct the imbalance before proceeding.

If you note a balance problem, first check to see if the crossbar [2] and the circular spar [1] frames are centered over the centerpole [3]. You can adjust the lashings to remedy any centering difficulties. If the balance problem persists, there is probably a weight differential on either side of the centerpole [3]. Whittle or pare or sandpaper the crossbar [2] and/or the circular spar [1] frames on the heavier side until the frame balances properly.

When the frame does balance properly, soak the string of all the lashings with glue, and then set the frame aside and allow it to dry.

Preparing The Kite Cover

YOU CAN USE either paper or a polyethylene fabric to cover the frame of the kite of circles. Suitable papers include newspaper, wrapping paper, tissue paper, shelf paper, brown paper, rice paper, and the imitation Japanese paper found at art supply stores.

After obtaining the cover material, place the kite frame on the kite cover [4] with the

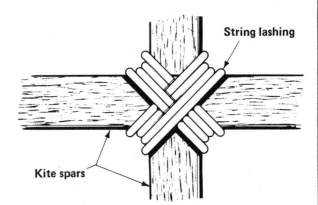

Lash the crossbar and centerpole together.

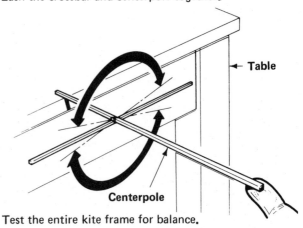

Test the entire kite frame for balance.

centerpole [3] side away from the cover. Then use a pencil to trace around the outside edge of one circular spar [1] frame, allowing a half-inch margin all around it. Later, you will glue this margin to enclose the frame.

Cut out the kite cover [4] with sharp scissors, and then check to be sure that it properly covers each of the other three circular spar [1] frames. If it does, cut three more identical circles, making any adjustment necessary to provide a suitable kite cover [4] for each; remember to allow the half-inch margin on every cover [4]. Finally, notch the edges of each circular kite covering [4] to allow for smooth folding.

At this point, you should take some time to decorate the kite cover [4]. You will find suggestions and guidelines for kite decorations in the chapter "Decorating the Kite," and you can get some specific ideas by studying the full-color illustration of the Kite Of Circles.

When you finish decorating the kite cover [4], attach it to the frame. First, crease the margin of one kite cover [4] over one of the circular spar [1] frames, completely enclosing it. Next, apply glue to the margin, and seal the margin over the circular spar [1] frame. Try to avoid wrinkles and creases which might later hinder flight. Follow the same procedure for attaching the other three kite covers [4] to the other three circular spar [1] frames.

The next step is to fasten on a simple two-legged bridle, which will control the angle at which the surface of the kite meets the wind. First, with a nail or sharp-pointed tool, carefully punch a hole in the center of the top circle's kite cover [4], directly over the centerpole [3]. Next, carefully punch a second hole at the center of the bottom circle, again directly over the centerpole [3]. Apply a notebook reinforcer to each hole to prevent tearing of the kite cover [4].

Now, cut a piece of bridle string [5] equal in length to the total length of both the centerpole [3] and the crossbar [2] — 80 inches in this case. Guide one end of the bridle string [5] through the hole at the top of the kite, and tie it securely to the centerpole [3]. Loop the other end of the bridle string [5] two or three times through a bridle ring (a curtain ring is suitable), and then guide it through the hole at the bottom of the kite before tying it securely to the centerpole [3]. Adjust the placement of the

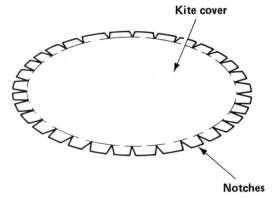

Notch the edges of each circular kite covering.

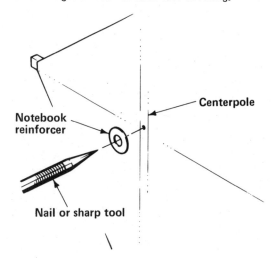

Punch holes in the kite cover for the bridle string.

bridle ring by sliding it along the bridle string [5] until it is directly above the center of the entire kite. When you have the bridle ring properly adjusted, wrap a small piece of adhesive tape around the ring to hold the bridle string [5] secure.

The final step in creating a kite of circles is to glue a paper streamer or fabric tail [6] — necessary to stabilize the kite in flight — to the bottom end of the centerpole [3]. The paper streamer (crepe or tissue paper) is more popular than the fabric tail for the kite of circles. The exact length of the tail [6] must be appropriate to the prevailing wind conditions, but an average tail [6] should be approximately four to five times the length of the centerpole [3]. Flight-test the kite and then adjust the tail [6] accordingly. If the kite tends to loop and spin in flight, lengthen the tail [6]. If the tail appears to restrict the kite's movement, shorten it.

The Kite of Circles   Scale: Grid Squares = 1″ (except as noted)

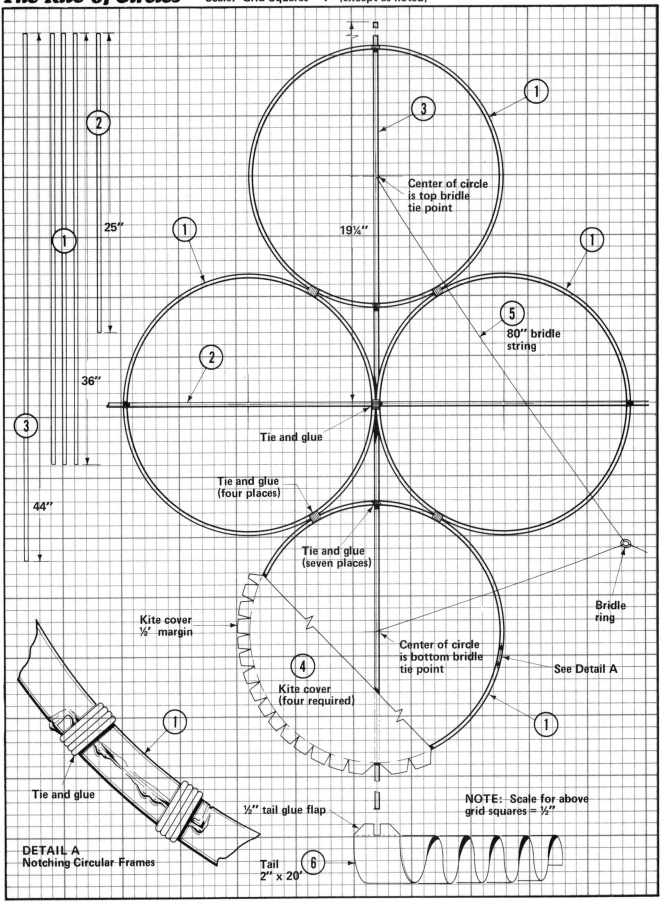

2

1

25″

1

3

36″

2

44″

3

1

3

Center of circle is top bridle tie point

19¼″

1

5

80″ bridle string

1

Tie and glue

Tie and glue (four places)

Tie and glue (seven places)

Bridle ring

Kite cover ½′ margin

4

Kite cover (four required)

Center of circle is bottom bridle tie point

See Detail A

1

Tie and glue

1

½″ tail glue flap

NOTE: Scale for above grid squares = ½″

DETAIL A
Notching Circular Frames

Tail 2″ x 20′

6

68

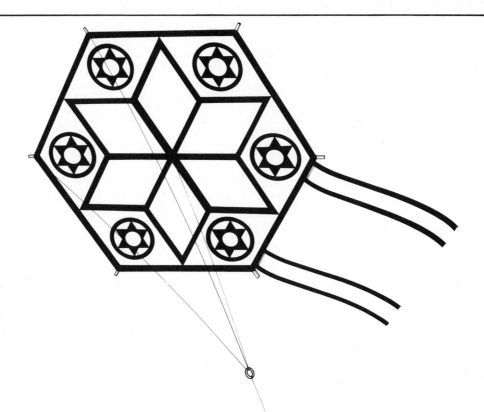

The Hexagonal Kite

THE THREE-SPAR hexagonal kite is another flat kite, but it is slightly more complex in construction than most flat kites. A three-spar kite can have spars of equal or unequal length; hexagonal three-spar kites, however, always have three spars of equal length.

Hexagonal three-spar kites provide the opportunity for more interesting decoration than do most two-spar kites. In Bermuda — where three-spar kites are very popular — they are usually covered with brightly colored tissue paper elaborately decorated with cut and pasted designs. In China, these kites are often decorated to resemble the faces of wild-eyed warriors.

The directions that follow are for the traditional Chinese hexagonal kite. It is a strong kite that flies very well. The measurements given here are in terms of proportion, but you should use spars that are at least two feet in length for good flight stability.

Kite Frame Materials

BEGIN BY selecting the proper frame material. Split bamboo is ideal because it is strong and light. You may find all the split bamboo you need for this kite frame in discarded outdoor porch shades. If you cannot obtain bamboo, however, you can fashion the spars from square-sectioned hardwood or softwood available at most hobby or lumber stores.

How To Create A Hexagonal Kite

FIRST CUT three spars [1] of exactly equal lengths. Now test each spar [1] for balance, by carefully measuring and marking the exact

> **Editor's Note:** The numbers and detail citations that appear in brackets [ ] throughout this chapter refer to the scale drawing of The Hexagonal Kite.

center of each spar [1] and then balancing the spar [1] at this mark on the edge of a knife blade. If one side tends to go down, the spar [1] is not balanced and you must correct the imbalance by whittling or sandpapering the heavier side until the spar balances properly.

When you are satisfied that each spar is balanced, use a sharp knife or a saw to cut notches in both ends of all three spars [1]. These notches will later hold the kite's guideline string [2]. Notching, however, can cause the wood to split when pressure is applied. To prevent splitting, lash the spar [1] with string just below the notch.

You are now ready to join the spars [1] together. Place one of the spars [1] on a flat surface, and position a second spar [1] over the first to form an "X." The spars must touch at their exact centers. Next, place the third spar horizontally across the "X" so that the joint formed at the center marking of each spar [1] creates six identical angles.

When you get the spars [1] correctly positioned, lash the point of juncture with string [Detail A]. The string you use for this purpose should be strong, should not stretch, and should not add bulk; a common four-ply cotton string is quite suitable. In lashing the spars [1] together, make at least two turns through each angle, and then weave the string over and under the point of juncture. Tie the string with a square knot, and clip off any excess.

Now test the balance of the entire kite frame. It is important that the frame balance on both sides of each spar [1] since each spar [1] acts as a centerpole when the kite is rotated. In order to check the kite frame's balance, place one end of a spar [1] on a table and the other end of the same spar [1] on the tip of your finger. The frame should rest along a horizontal plane. If the frame tends to dip to one side, you must correct the imbalance before proceeding further.

First measure to be certain that the spars [1] are joined at their exact centers. Next, measure to be sure that all six angles at the point of juncture are equal. Make adjustments — if any — as indicated. If the imbalance persists, check the weight distribution of each spar [1]. If one has a heavier side, whittle or sandpaper it until the frame balances as it should. Finally rotate the frame and, using each spar [1] as a centerpole, test for balance at every position.

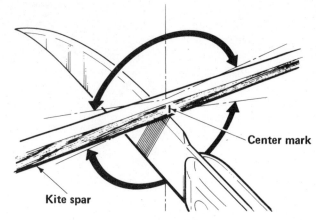

Balance the spars on a knife blade's edge.

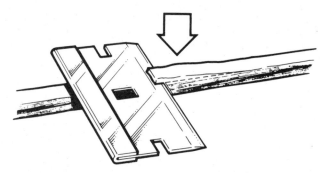

Trim down the heavier side to correct a spar's imbalance.

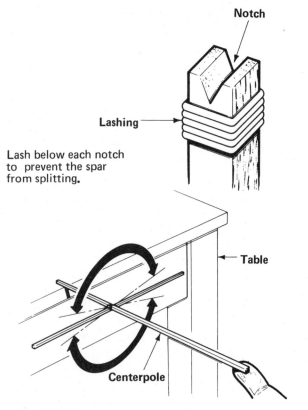

Lash below each notch to prevent the spar from splitting.

Test the balance of the entire kite frame.

When you are satisfied that the frame is balanced, apply glue to the lashing. Any quick-drying glue that becomes tough rather than brittle is appropriate. Be sure, however, that you use enough glue to soak the string of the joints and knots thoroughly. Now set the frame aside and allow it to dry.

The next step is to frame the spars [1] with a guideline string [2]. This will make a firm edge on which to mount the kite cover, and it will enable the kite to maintain its shape during flight. Use string that possesses at least the same strength as you used to lash the joints. Attach the guideline string [2] to the notch at the end of one of the spars [1] by knotting it securely. Then stretch the string on to the next spar [1] — keeping it taut at all times — and tie it in the same manner. Continue on around the frame until you get back to where you started; then tie the two ends of the string together.

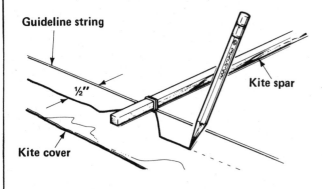

Trace around the outside edge of the guideline string, leaving a half-inch margin all around.

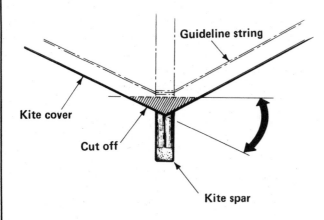

Mark notches where each of the spars will protrude.

Preparing The Kite Cover

YOU ARE NOW ready to prepare the covering for the hexagonal three-spar kite. Select a covering material that is both lightweight and strong. Paper is a popular cover material for the hexagonal kite, although lightweight fabric is also fully acceptable — as long as the material used is not so porous that it would allow the wind to blow through it. Wrapping paper, tissue paper, newspaper, shelf paper, brown paper, rice paper, or even imitation Japanese paper (available at art supply stores) are all suitable for the kite cover [3].

Lay the kite frame on top of the kite cover [3], and trace around the outside edge of the frame (the guideline string [2]) with a pencil, leaving a half-inch margin all around. The margin provides the overlap you will later glue around the guideline string [2] frame. Before you cut the shape out with sharp scissors, though, you must mark notches where each of the spars will protrude. Then cut the kite cover [3] and slit each of the six corners one-half inch to allow for neat folding over the guideline string [2].

At this point, with the kite cover [3] cut to size, you can decorate the kite. For tips and suggestions, refer to the chapter "Decorating the Kite"; for ideas, examine the full-color illustration of the Hexagonal Kite.

After decorating the kite cover [3] and making certain that both it and the glue on the frame are thoroughly dry, position the frame on top of the undecorated side of the kite cover [3]. Then crease and glue the margin over the guideline string [2] frame. Try to avoid wrinkles and creases as you seal the margin with the guideline string [2] securely inside. If you have a fabric kite cover [3], either glue or sew it with a running stitch; be sure to wait until the glue is completely dry before proceeding.

The next step is to prepare a three-legged bridle, which is necessary to control the angle at which the surface of the kite meets the wind. First, measure the perimeter around any one of the six triangles formed by the frame of the kite. Next, cut a piece of bridle string [4] to a length that is twice this perimeter measurement and another length of bridle string [5] four-fifths this perimeter measurement. Then take the longer bridle string [4] and tie it securely to the exposed end of one spar [1]. Loop the other end of the bridle string [4] two

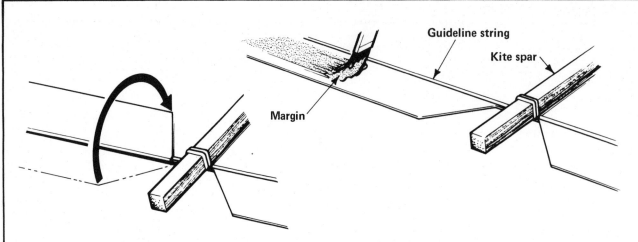

Crease and glue the margin of the kite cover over the guideline string frame.

or three times through a bridle ring — a curtain ring can be used for this purpose — and tie this end to the spar [1] that is directly adjacent to the spar [1] to which you just tied the first end of the bridle string [4]. Position the bridle ring midway on the length of bridle string [4].

Now, with a nail or a sharp-pointed tool, carefully punch a hole through the kite cover [3] just above the center of the kite frame. Apply a notebook reinforcer around the hole to prevent tearing. Tie one end of the shorter bridle string [5] to the bridle ring, and guide the other end through the reinforced hole. Tie it to the center of the kite frame, but do not trim the excess bridle string [5] because you may need it later — after the kite has become airborne — for adjustment purposes.

The final step is to prepare the tail [6]. A hexagonal kite usually has two tails [6] generally made of crepe paper or tissue paper, but it has no strips on these tails [6] because a double tail with strips might tend to tangle.

To make the tail [6] for a hexagonal kite, cut two paper streamers each of which is at least twice as long as one of the frame spars [1]. Attach the tails [6] by gluing them at a position near the two lower spars [1] of the kite frame. Do not tie them on.

You may need to adjust the tail later so that it provides stability by its weight as well as its air resistance. Varying wind conditions can necessitate such adjustments. For example, if the kite tends to loop and spin, you must lengthen the tails. You must shorten the tails, though, if they seem to restrict the kite's movement.

There is also another type of tail [7] that can be used with the hexagonal kite. It consists of two leader lines [8] and a single tail [7]. Each of the leader lines [8] must be at least three times the length of one of the kite's spars [1]. You attach (glue) the leader lines [8] at the same positions as you would the two tails [6] just described. Then you connect the leader lines [8] to one long tail [7], which should be fringed to increase air resistance. The hexagonal three-spar kites so popular in Bermuda often have tails as long as 25 feet.

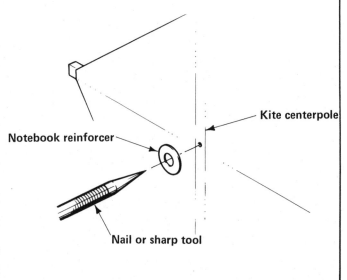

Punch a hole in the kite cover for the bridle string.

The Hexagonal Kite   Scale: Grid Squares = ½″

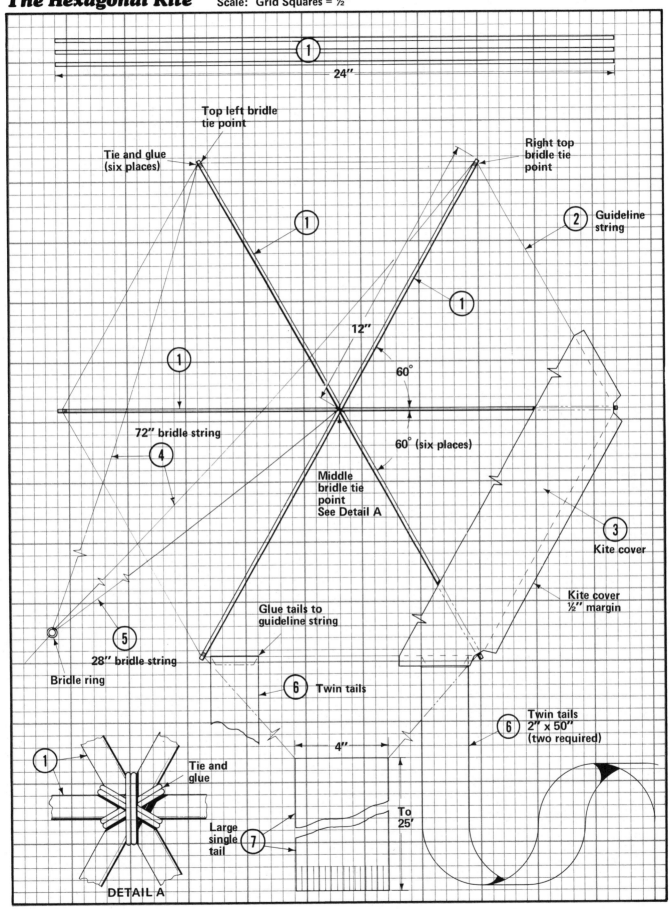

(1)

24″

Top left bridle tie point

Tie and glue (six places)

Right top bridle tie point

(1)

(2) Guideline string

(1)

12″

60°

(1)

72″ bridle string

(4)

60° (six places)

Middle bridle tie point See Detail A

(3)

Kite cover

Kite cover ½″ margin

Glue tails to guideline string

(5)

28″ bridle string

Bridle ring

(6) Twin tails

Twin tails 2″ x 50″ (two required)

(6)

4″

(1)

Tie and glue

To 25′

Large single tail

(7)

DETAIL A

The Bird Kite

THE BIRD KITES, among the most representational of all kites, have enjoyed
great popularity for centuries in both Asia and
the western world. Bird kites come in many
and various forms. Some are nothing more
than simple diamond kites decorated as birds,
while others are considerably more complex.
A few, like the compound bird kite, even have
wings that move separately from the body of
the kite.

Although the following bird kite instructions include precise measurements, you
can make one that is smaller or larger as long
as you maintain the proper proportions.

Kite Frame Materials

TO CONSTRUCT the frame of this bird kite,
you will need three quarter-inch spars 30
inches long and a nine-inch strip of wood for
bracing. Birch dowels or quarter-inch
square-sectioned sticks of cypress, spruce, or
pine can be used for the spars. These lightweight but strong woods are readily available
at most lumber markets and hobby or
hardware stores.

One spar forms the centerpole [1] of the
bird kite, while the other are used as the wing
spars [2].

How To Create A Bird Kite

BEGIN BY notching both ends of the centerpole [1], but only one end of each of the
wing spars [2]. Since notching can cause the
wood to split when pressure is applied, lash
the spars with thread just below the notch and
then soak the thread thoroughly with glue. Be

Editor's Note: The numbers and detail citations that appear in brackets [ ] throughout this chapter refer to the
scale drawing of The Bird Kite.

sure to use a glue that dries quickly and becomes tough rather than brittle.

You attach the wing spars [2] to the centerpole [1] with a 1½-inch finishing nail. Drill a clearance hole through the centerpole [1] six inches from one end — the diameter of the hole should be the same as the diameter of the nail that will penetrate it — and lash the centerpole [1] with thread both above and below the hole to prevent splitting. Then thoroughly soak the thread with glue.

Now drill a hole one-half inch deep, using the same diameter drill bit as before, into the unnotched end of each of the wing spars [2]. Lash the end of each wing spar [2] with thread and then soak the thread with glue.

Next, cut the head off the 1½-inch finishing nail with a hacksaw, and file the end until it is smooth. Insert the headless nail into the hole that you drilled through the centerpole [1] so that it is perfectly centered; then apply glue to hold the nail in place. Wait until the glue is completely dry before proceeding to the next step.

You are now ready to push the wing spars [2] onto the ends of the nail [Detail A]. When you finish, apply glue to hold these spars securely.

Now is the time to test the kite frame for balance. It is crucial that the kite frame balance on either side of the centerpole [1]. In order to test for balance, place one end of the centerpole [1] on the edge of a table and lay the other end on the tip of your finger. The entire frame should rest evenly along a horizontal plane.

If the frame tends to dip to one side, however, it must be corrected before you can proceed any further in the construction of the bird kite. First check to be sure that the wing spars [2] are properly fitted on the nail ends. If they are, then the imbalance problem most likely stems from an unequal weight of the wing spars [2], and you should whittle or sandpaper the heavier side until the frame balances properly.

The next step is to wrap the wing spars [2] with a guideline string [3]. Later, this string [3] will provide a firm edge on which to mount the kite cover [5] as well as help the kite maintain its shape. Choosing the type of string for this purpose is not critical; a common four-ply cotton string is quite suitable. Whatever string you use, however, must be strong, and it

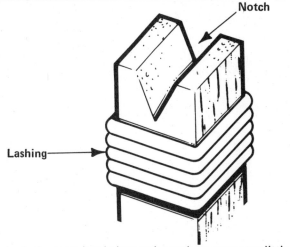

Lash the spars just below each notch to prevent splitting.

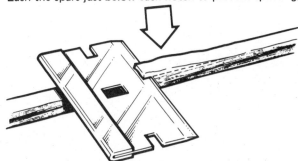

Pare down the heavier side of a spar so that it balances.

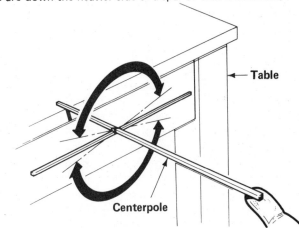

Test the entire kite frame for balance.

should not stretch or add bulk.

Attach the guideline string [3] to the notch at the top of the centerpole [1] by knotting it, and then run the guideline string [3] to the notch of the wing spar [2]. Make sure that you keep the guideline string [3] taut as you take it through the notch and loop it once around the spar before continuing to guide it around the frame.

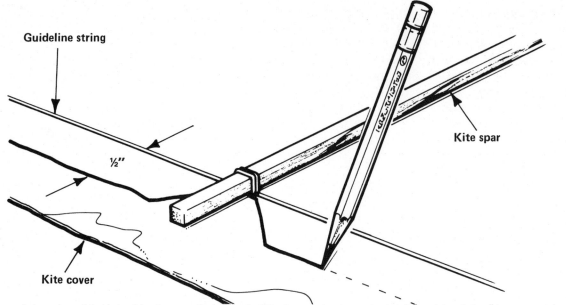

Guideline string

½"

Kite cover

Kite spar

Trace around the edge of half the kite frame, allowing a half-inch margin along the leading edge of the kite cover wings.

When you have completely framed the kite, tie the two ends of the guideline string [3] together without permitting any slack to occur. Do not cut off the excess string at this point because later adjustment of the lashing may be necessary.

Preparing The Kite Cover

THE NEXT STEP is to prepare a covering [5] for the bird kite. You will find it quite helpful if you first make a paper pattern to use when you actually cut the kite cover material. You will need a piece of paper 38 inches (vertical) by 62 inches (horizontal). Place the frame of the kite on the sheet of paper, and, with a pencil, trace around the edge of half of the kite frame, beginning at the head and ending at the tail. Use a compass and/or tin can to create the scalloped edges around the kite cover's wings and tail. Be sure to add a head flap [4] which extends six inches beyond the centerpole [1] in addition to a half-inch margin along the leading edge of the kite cover [5] wings. Now fold the paper in half, and — using sharp scissors — cut along the marking, producing a complete symmetrical pattern. Place the frame on the pattern once again, and check carefully to make certain that the pattern is shaped properly.

You can make the actual kite cover [5] from lightweight cloth like cotton or silk or from strong paper like wrapping paper, tissue paper, shelf paper, or brown paper. Using the paper pattern as a guide, carefully cut out the actual kite cover [5] with sharp scissors or a razor blade. If you select fabric for the covering, you would be wise to stitch all the edges — with the exception of the leading edge of the wings — with an overcast stitch in order to prevent fraying.

At this point, with the kite cover [5] cut to size, it is time to decorate the bird kite. If you wish to paint the kite cover [5], you can use watercolors or poster paints as well as water-thinned acrylic colors. Keep in mind that the paint you use should be lightweight, flexible, and quick-drying. For more elaborate bird kites, you can make the head of styrofoam, and then cover and shape it with paper maché. Fringed tissue paper or actual feathers can also be added to give a strikingly realistic appearance. For additional suggestions and tips on how to decorate the kite, refer to the chapter "Decorating the Kite" and to the full-color illustration of the Bird Kite.

When you are finished decorating and the kite cover [5] is thoroughly dry, you are ready to secure the wing spars [2] at a permanent dihedral angle. First notch both ends of the nine-inch cross-brace [6] so that it will lie flatly over the wing spars [2]. Next, center the cross-brace [6] over the point where the centerpole [1] and wing spars [2] are joined. Carefully bend the wing spars [2] back to form a slight "V" shape, which will produce a dihedral angle. In so doing, the nail will bend slightly.

Now use string to lash both ends of the cross-brace [6] to the wing spars [2], producing a permanent dihedral angle. Then soak the string with glue and allow it to dry thoroughly before proceeding. Check to be sure that the string guideline [3] around the kite frame is sufficiently taut, and make any adjustments before clipping off the excess string.

The next step is to attach the kite cover [5] to the frame. Place the frame on the undecorated side of the kite cover [5], with the centerpole [1] against the covering [5] and the wing spars [2] above it. Crease the margin along the leading edge of the wings and then glue the margin securely over the guideline string [3]. If you have a fabric covering, stitch the margin with thread so that the guideline string [3] is housed securely inside the pocket formed by the overlap.

Now secure the top of the centerpole [1] to the kite cover [5] by applying cloth tape [7] or a waterproof masking tape. Repeat this process at the bottom of the centerpole and then at both wing tips.

The final step is to secure the guideline string [3] in position along the backside of the wings and the tail, using two-inch strips of cloth tape at seven-inch intervals.

The only thing that the bird kite needs now before it is ready to fly is a bridle. The bridle is necessary to control the angle at which the surface of the kite meets the wind. Begin by carefully punching a hole with a nail or a sharp-pointed tool a quarter-inch from the leading edge of each wing at a point 11 inches in from each wing tip. If the kite cover is fabric, you can simply sink an eyelet [8] at this point, but if the covering is paper, apply a notebook reinforcer or tape [7] to prevent tearing.

Now cut a piece of bridle string [9] 55 inches long, and guide one end of the string through the hole and tie it securely to the kite cover [5] with the string guideline [3] inside. Loop the other end of the bridle string [9] two or three times through the first of two bridle rings — a curtain ring serves the purpose — and then run the loose end of the bridle string [9] through the hole on the other wing and tie it securely in the same manner. Slide the bridle ring to a position that is halfway between the two tied ends.

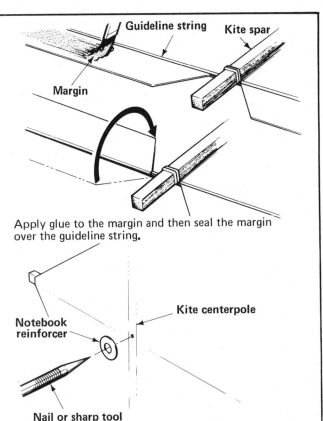

Apply glue to the margin and then seal the margin over the guideline string.

Punch holes in the kite cover for the bridle string.

Now cut another piece of bridle string [10] 42 inches long. If the kite cover [5] is fabric, sink an eyelet [8] approximately two inches down from the tip of the kite's head. If the cover material is paper, first reinforce the area with tape and then punch a hole at the point where the eyelet would have gone. Make another hole in the same fashion one-half inch up from the bottom of the tail. Then run one end of the bridle string [10] through the hole at the tip of the head and tie it securely to the covering. Loop the other end of the bridle string [10] two or three times through the second bridle ring, and then guide the loose end through the hole at the bottom of the kite and tie it securely to the bottom end of the centerpole [1]. Position this second bridle ring so that it is 13 inches from the tie at the top of the kite and 29 inches from the tie at the bottom. Both bridle rings should be attached to the same kite-flying line when you are ready to launch the bird kite.

This size bird kite flies best in a moderate to strong breeze. Generally, it will not function well at great heights and, therefore, it should be flown only at low to medium altitudes.

The Bird Kite Scale: Grid Squares = 1" (except as noted)

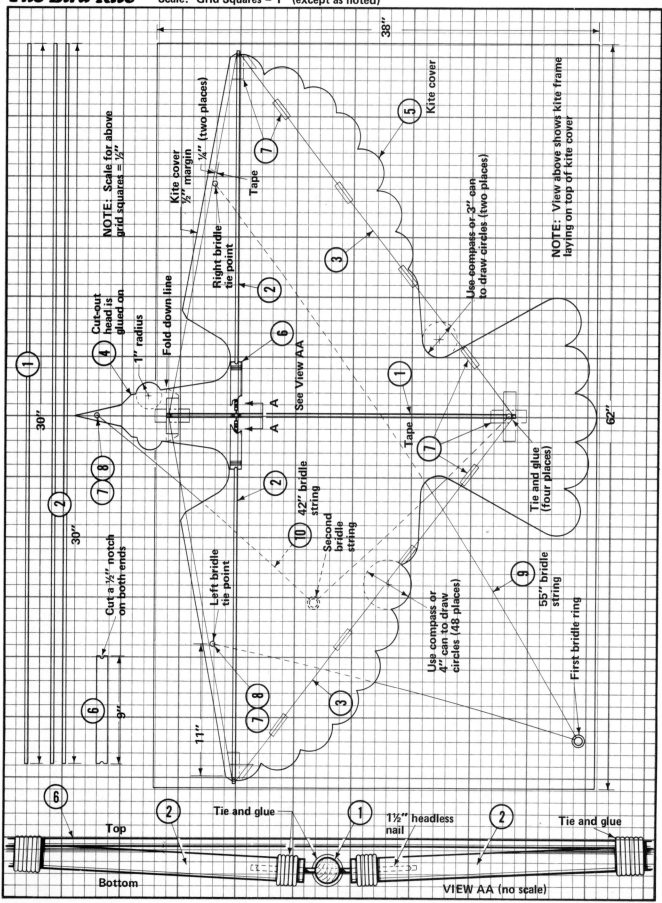

NOTE: Scale for above grid squares = ½"

Kite cover ½" margin

¼" (two places)

Tape

Right bridle tie point

Cut-out head is glued on

1" radius

Fold down line

See View AA

A
A

Kite cover

Use compass or 3" can to draw circles (two places)

NOTE: View above shows kite frame laying on top of kite cover

30"

30"

Cut a ½" notch on both ends

9"

Left bridle tie point

11"

42" bridle string

Second bridle string

Use compass or 4" can to draw circles (48 places)

Tape

Tie and glue (four places)

62"

55" bridle string

First bridle ring

Top

Tie and glue

1½" headless nail

Bottom

Tie and glue

VIEW AA (no scale)

38"

The Snake Kite

T HE SNAKE, or serpent, kite is an exotic though popular design that originated in Thailand. With its long tail flowing out from behind the relatively small flat kite that forms the snake's head, it creates a most unusual and dramatic sight in the sky.

The following directions are for the most traditional type of snake kite, one that has an arch-top spar. Snake kites can also be made with various other flat shapes forming the snake's face, and, of course, they can be altered considerably in appearance through innovative decorating techniques.

Kite Frame Materials

SPLIT BAMBOO is the ideal material for constructing the snake kite frame. Not only is it both strong and lightweight, but bamboo also can be bent into a specific shape and it will retain that shape permanently. While you can buy split bamboo at most craft stores and hobby shops, you may find just what you need for a snake kite frame in discarded outdoor porch shades. Or, you can simply split your own from old bamboo poles or canes. Just

make sure that the material you use is no larger that a quarter-inch square.

You will need three spars to form the frame of the snake kite: one 12-inch spar to form the centerpole [1], one 10-inch spar to

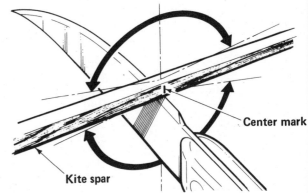

Balance the spar at its center point on the edge of a knife blade.

Editor's Note: The numbers and detail citations that appear in brackets [ ] throughout this chapter refer to the scale drawing of The Snake Kite.

form the crossbar [2], and a 32-inch spar to form the arch-top [3] of the frame. The exact measurements of these spars can vary, providing that the proportions given here are maintained.

How To Create A Snake Kite

THE FIRST thing to do is test each of the spars [1, 2, and 3] for balance. Mark the exact center of each spar with a pencil line, and then balance the spar at this point on the edge of a knife blade. If one side tends to go down, correct the imbalance by whittling or sandpapering the heavier side. Proper balance is a crucial requirement for successful kite-making.

When you are satisfied that all the spars [1, 2, and 3] are properly balanced, you are ready to prepare the 32-inch arch-top spar [3] so that it will bend without splitting.

You can prepare the arch-top spar [3] one of two ways. Either soak it in water for approximately two hours, after which it should be nicely flexible, or — a much quicker method — move the arch-top spar [3] back and forth over a candle flame, applying pressure to bend it into the proper shape. Be careful, however, not to hold the bamboo motionless over the flame because you could burn or deform it, thereby losing it as a framing spar.

When the arch-top spar [3] is sufficiently flexible, attach it to the centerpole [1]. The point of juncture should be at the exact center of the arch-top spar [3] about a quarter-inch down from the top of the centerpole [1]. First lay these two spars [1 and 3] in the correct position, and then lash them together with string. The type of string you use for this purpose is not critical; a common four-ply cotton string is quite suitable. Whatever string you use, however, should be strong, should not stretch, should not add bulk, and should be a minimum of eight inches in length.

Lash the arch-top spar [3] and the centerpole [1] in position by taking at least two turns through both diagonals at the point of juncture. Then weave the string over and under, and tie it with a square knot. Clip off any excess string.

The next step involves bowing the arch-top spar [3]. Cut a piece of string [4] to a length of 20 inches, and lash one end of the string securely to one end of the arch-top spar [3]. Now take the other end of the string [4]

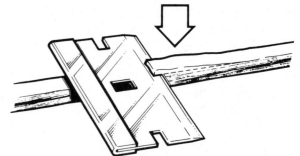

Pare down any bumps or irregularities affecting the spar's balance.

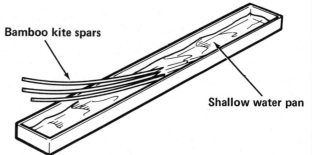

Bamboo kite spars

Shallow water pan

Soak the spars in water for two hours to make them flexible.

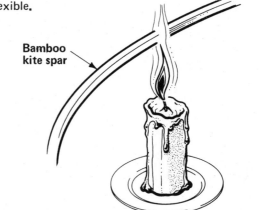

Bamboo kite spar

Move the spar back and forth over a candle flame until it bends properly.

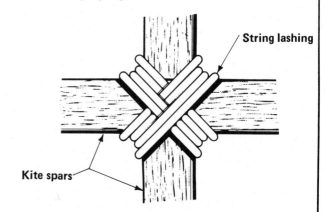

String lashing

Kite spars

Lash the arch-top spar and centerpole together by weaving the string over and under both diagonals at the point of juncture.

and tie it securely to the other end of the arch-top spar [3], bowing the spar until the distance between its two ends is 15 inches. Lash the string [4] securely when the arch-top spar [3] reaches the proper degree of bow, and trim away any excess string.

You are now ready to attach the crossbar spar [2] that supports the snake kite. Position the crossbar spar [2] two inches down from the top of the centerpole [1]. The center mark on the crossbar spar [2] should be directly over the centerpole [1], and the ends of the crossbar should overlap the ends of the bowed arch-top spar [3]. Now lash the crossbar spar [2] to the centerpole [1] with string, taking at least two turns through both diagonals, and then weave the string over and under before tying it securely with a square knot and clipping off any excess string. Finally, attach each end of the crossbar spar [2] to the bowed arch-top spar [3] with string, following the same lashing procedure described for fastening the crossbar spar [2] to the centerpole [1].

Now test the entire kite frame for balance; it is very important that the kite frame balance precisely on either side of the centerpole [1]. In order to test the kite frame for balance, place one end of the centerpole on the edge of a table and rest the other end on the tip of your finger. The entire frame should rest along a horizontal plane. If the frame tends to dip to one side, it is not balanced, and you must correct the problem before proceeding any further in the construction. To find the cause of the imbalance, first check to be sure that the centerpole [1] actually intersects the exact centers of the crossbar spar [2] and the arch-top spar [3]. If it does not, adjust the lashing until it does. If the frame still fails to balance, the cause is probably the unequal weight of the sides of the crossbar spar [2] and/or the arch-top spar [3]. To correct this situation, whittle or sandpaper the heavier side until the kite frame balances as it should.

When the frame balances, apply glue to all the lashings. Any glue that dries quickly and becomes tough rather than brittle is suitable for this job. Be sure that you use enough glue, however, to soak each string and knot thoroughly.

Now set the kite frame aside and allow it to dry. When it is dry, you will have a strong, balanced frame on which to construct the snake kite.

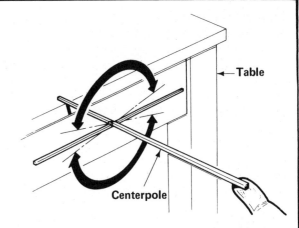

Test the kite frame for balance by placing one end of the centerpole on the edge of a table and the other end on the tip of your finger.

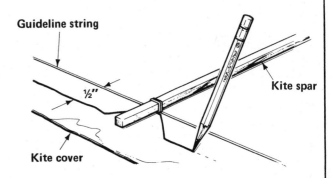

Place the kite frame on the kite cover and trace around the frame, allowing a half-inch margin all the way around.

Preparing The Kite Cover

YOU ARE NOW ready to prepare the covering [5] for the snake kite. Silk is the traditional covering material for this kite, but silk is so expensive that it may be prudent to substitute another material. The covering selected must, however, be both lightweight and strong. Tissue paper, crepe paper, wrapping paper, or Mylar will make a fine covering for a snake kite; rice paper or imitation Japanese paper (available at art supply stores) will also work very well.

After selecting the cover material, place the kite frame on the kite cover [5] with the centerpole [1] side away from the covering. Trace around the outside edge of the frame with a pencil (be sure to include the string [4] along the bottom of the arch-top spar [3]), allowing a half-inch margin all around the kite frame. Later, you will glue this margin to enclose the frame. Finally, cut out the kite cover [5] with sharp scissors, notching the edges of the cover on the curved sides to allow for smooth folding.

This is the time to decorate the kite cover to your own specifications. Refer to the suggestions and guidelines in the chapter "Decorating the Kite" and to the full-color illustration of the Snake Kite. The most common form of decoration is to paint a snake's head on the entire surface of the flat kite; the snake's long body, actually the kite's tail, will be attached to the kite frame later.

When you finish decorating the kite cover [5] — and the paint is dry — you must attach it to the kite frame. Crease the margin of the covering [5] over the frame, completely enclosing it. Then apply glue to the margin and seal it over the bamboo and string frame. Try to avoid wrinkles and creases which might later hinder flight.

The next step is to prepare a bridle for the snake kite. A simple, two-legged bridle is quite sufficient for controlling the angle at which the surface of the kite meets the air flow. First, use a nail or sharp-pointed tool to punch a hole in the kite cover directly over the point of juncture formed by the centerpole [1] and the crossbar spar [2]. Next, punch a second hole over the centerpole [1] about one inch above the bottom end of the centerpole [1]. If you are using paper as the kite cover material, apply a notebook reinforcer around each hole to prevent tearing.

Now cut a piece of bridle string [6] 23 inches long. Guide one end of the bridle string [6] through the hole at the top of the kite, and tie it securely to the centerpole [1].

Take the other end of the string and loop it two or three times through a bridle ring (a curtain ring will serve the purpose). Then guide the other end of the bridle string [6] through the hole at the bottom of the kite, and tie it securely to the centerpole [1]. Adjust the placement of the bridle ring by sliding it along the bridle string [6] until it is in a position directly above the center of the entire kite. When the bridle ring is properly adjusted, wrap a small piece of adhesive tape around the ring to hold the bridle string [6] secure.

The final step in creating a snake kite — and perhaps the most important in terms of

dramatic effect — is to prepare the tail [7] which forms the snake's long body. Make the tail of tissue paper or half-mil Mylar; any heavier material will tend to weight down the kite since the tail [7] itself is between 25 and 35 feet long. To start with, fashion a tail [7] that is 35 feet long; after a test flight, you can always shorten it if it overly restricts the kite's movement. The width of the tail [7] at the top should be about 15 inches, but this width should taper so that the tail [7] gradually slims down to about four inches wide at the end.

After cutting the tail [7] to its proper size, you should attach a strip of strapping tape down the center of its full length to serve as a reinforcement. Then decorate the tail [7] of the kite to make it compatible with the snake's head. The last step is simply to attach the tail [7] to the kite by gluing it securely in place along the bottom of the kite frame.

The unique snake kite is now ready to fly. At its best in light to moderate winds, the snake kite provides a spectacular sight in the sky, and it is an easy kite to control and retrieve.

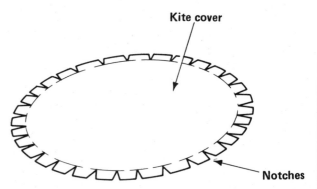

Notch the edge of the kite cover on the curved sides to facilitate folding.

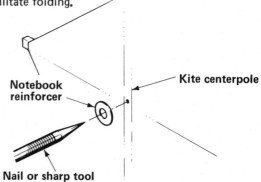

Punch holes in the kite cover to accommodate the bridle string. If the kite cover is paper, apply a notebook reinforcer around every hole.

The Snake Kite

Scale: Grid Squares = ½″

The Chinese Butterfly Kite

JUST AS BIRDS and airplanes lend their shapes well to kite designs, so does the butterfly. Not only is the butterfly a popular design, but it is also one that allows for a startling variety of decorations. Many ordinary kites can be decorated to look like butterflies, but this kite resembles a butterfly in its construction as well as its coloring.

A traditional Chinese design, the butterfly kite is a rather basic kite to construct. It is a common flat kite, but it offers wonderful possibilities for exceptionally beautiful decoration.

Kite Frame Materials

SPLIT BAMBOO is an ideal material for the frame of the butterfly kite. Strong and lightweight, bamboo can be curved or bent and it will retain its shape. Split bamboo is available at most craft stores and hobby shops, but you can usually get the bamboo you need for kite frames from discarded outdoor or porch shades; they are generally made of bamboo that is already split. Another way to obtain material for kite frames is simply to split your own from an old bamboo pole or cane. The split bamboo spars you need should be no larger than one-quarter inch square.

You will need four spars to construct the frame of the butterfly kite. An 18-inch spar [1] will form the spine or centerpole of the kite frame, while a 48-inch spar [2] will form the tail section of the butterfly. Two 24-inch spars [3] will be used to form the wing sections of the butterfly kite.

> **Editor's Note:** The numbers and detail citations that appear in brackets [ ] throughout this chapter refer to the scale drawing of The Chinese Butterfly Kite.

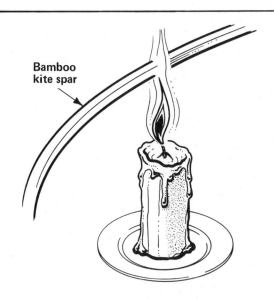

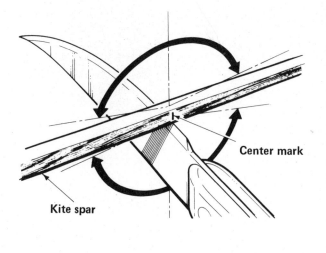

Move the spar over a candle flame while bending it.

Balance the spar on the edge of a knife.

How To Create A Butterfly Kite

FIRST, YOU MUST test the spars — after cutting each to exact size — for proper balance. This is done by making a pencil mark at the center of each spar and then balancing the spar at this point on the edge of a knife blade. If one side tends to go down, the spar is not balanced. You can correct any balance problem easily by whittling or sandpapering the heavier side until the spar balances properly on the knife blade. All the spars must balance perfectly for the kite to be a success.

When you are satisfied that the spars are balanced, you must bend the three longest spars [2 and 3]. If you soak the spars in water for about two hours, they will become so pliable that you can bend them easily without

their splitting or cracking. Or you can move each spar back and forth over a candle flame, applying pressure to the spar so that it curves into the shape desired. Be careful, however, not to hold the piece of bamboo motionless over the flame because it could burn or become permanently deformed.

When you are ready to begin constructing the kite frame, lay the 18-inch spar [1], which will be the centerpole, on a flat surface. Then taper each end of the 48-inch tail spar [2] to facilitate lashing [Detail A]. Now place the tail spar [2] in position over the centerpole [1] so that the centermark on the tail spar is directly over and six inches up from the bottom of the centerpole [1].

The next step involves lashing the two spars [1 and 2] in position at their point of

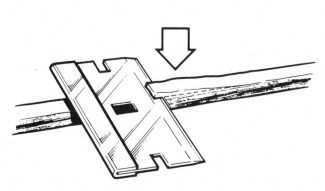

Pare the spar's heavier side until balance is achieved.

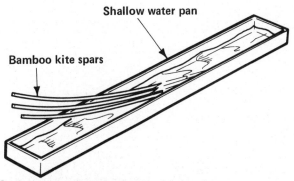

Soak the spars in water before shaping them.

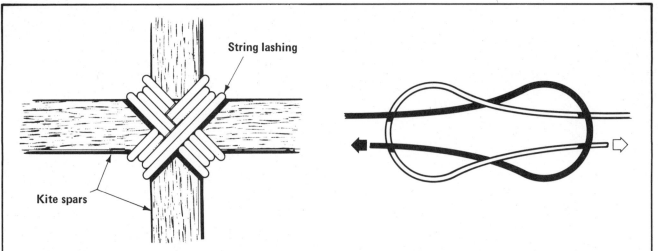

(LEFT) Lash the centerpole and tail spar together by wrapping their point of juncture with string. (RIGHT) Tie the string ends into a square knot.

juncture. Use string that is strong and that will neither stretch nor add bulk. A common four-ply cotton string is quite suitable for this lashing. Make at least two turns with the string through both diagonals of the crossing point, and then weave the string over and under the sticks. Finally, tie the ends with a square knot and clip off any excess string.

Now gently bend one end of the tail spar [2] until the tapered end overlaps and is parallel to the centerpole below the joint [Detail A]. Bring the other end of the tail spar [2] around to join the bottom of the centerpole [1], forming an identical loop. Now lash the joints securely with string. When tying two surfaces that run parallel, it is best to make two lashings that are as far apart as possible [Detail A]. Tie a square knot at each point of lashing.

The next step is to attach the 24-inch wing spars [3]. Taper one end of each of the wing spars [3] so that a smooth joint can be formed when it is joined to the curved tail spar [2]. Notch the other end of each wing spar [3] [Detail B].

Now take one of the 24-inch wing spars [3] and place it in position about 11 inches from the bottom of the centerpole [1] with the tapered edge joining the curved tail spar [2] [Detail C]. Secure the end of this wing spar [3] to the curved tail spar [2] by again making two lashings as far apart as possible.

Position the second 24-inch wing spar [3] to form the opposite side of the butterfly frame, and lash the end of it to the curved tail spar [2]. Carefully measure this wing spar [3] to make sure that the length it extends beyond the centerpole is identical to that of the first wing spar [3]. This will help to prevent any imbalance.

When you are sure that the wing spars [3] are positioned evenly, lash the joint formed by the two wing spars [3] and the centerpole [1] with string. Make at least two turns with the string through each diagonal of the crossing point, and then weave the string over and under the spars. Finally, tie the ends with a square knot and clip off any excess string.

To complete the kite frame, you must attach a string guideline. Cut two 18-inch lengths of string [4] and tie one end of one piece of string securely to the end of one notched wing spar [3]. Now pull the string [4] gently, bending the wing spar [3] downward until it forms the desired shape. Then tie the string securely to the curved tail spar [2]. Repeat this process on the opposite side of the kite frame, making both sides identical to insure that proper balance is maintained. Now tie a 14-inch piece of string [5] from the top of the centerpole [1] to each of the wing spars [3] to form the frame for the head of the butterfly.

At this point the entire kite frame, as constructed, should be tested for balance. It is critically important that the frame balance precisely on either side of the centerpole [1]. In order to test for balance, place one end of the centerpole [1] on a table and rest the other end on the tip of your finger, balancing the frame on a horizontal plane. If it remains in this position, the frame is in balance. If the frame tends to dip to one side, however, it is not

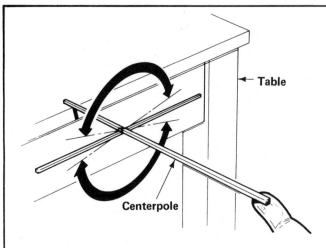

Test the entire kite frame for balance.

properly balanced and you must correct it before proceeding any further.

To determine the cause of the imbalance, first measure to make certain that proportions are equal on both sides of the centerpole [1]. If they are not, make the necessary adjustments. If this does not correct the imbalance, the problem undoubtedly lies in the unequal weight of one or more of the spars. Pare or sandpaper the heavier side until the kite frame balances properly.

When you are satisfied that the frame is in balance, apply glue to all the lashings. Any glue that dries quickly and becomes tough rather than brittle is appropriate for this job. Be sure, however, that you use enough glue to soak the string of the joints and knots thoroughly. Set the frame aside now until the

glue is completely dry, at which time you will have a sturdy frame on which to build the butterfly kite.

Preparing The Kite Cover

THE NEXT STEP is to prepare the kite cover. The cover material must be both lightweight and strong. Any strong, durable paper (wrapping paper, tissue paper, rice paper, or imitation Japanese paper) will work very nicely to cover the butterfly kite.

Begin by placing the kite frame on the kite cover, with the centerpole [1] of the frame away from the covering. With a pencil, trace an outline around the outside edge of the bamboo and string frame, providing for a one-inch margin all around. Later, you will wrap and glue this margin around the frame. When you are finished tracing the pattern, cut out the kite cover using sharp scissors to get a clean, neat cutting edge. You will find it helpful later in folding the cover around the kite frame if you cut small notches in the one-inch margin around the pattern.

Now, with the covering cut to size, it is time to decorate. Refer to the chapter "Decorating The Kite" and to the full-color illustration of the Chinese Butterfly Kite for ideas.

When the kite is decorated and completely dry, it is time to glue the kite cover to the frame. Crease the cover margin over the frame to provide a guideline. Then apply glue to the margin and seal it securely around the frame itself. Try your best to avoid wrinkles and creases as you wrap and glue the kite

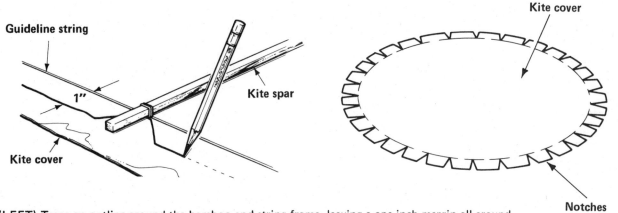

(LEFT) Trace an outline around the bamboo and string frame, leaving a one-inch margin all around.
(RIGHT) Cut small notches in the kite cover's margin to facilitate folding.

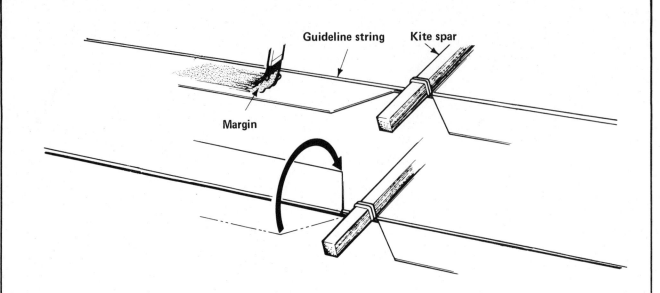

Guideline string   Kite spar

Margin

Apply glue to the margin and seal it securely around the frame.

cover. At this point, you can attach two pipe cleaners [6] to the centerpole [1] to resemble feelers.

You must now prepare a bridle, which will control the angle at which the surface of the kite meets the wind. A simple, two-legged bridle is sufficient for the butterfly kite. First, with a nail or other sharp object carefully punch a hole in the kite cover above the point of juncture where the wing spars [3] cross the

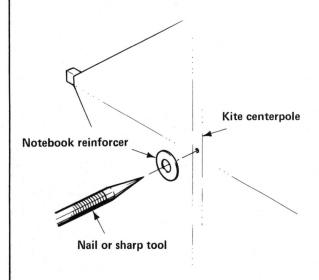

Kite centerpole

Notebook reinforcer

Nail or sharp tool

Punch holes in the kite cover for the bridle strings.

centerpole [1]. Punch a second hole — just as carefully — slightly above the bottom of the centerpole [1]. If the cover material is paper, apply a notebook reinforcer to each hole to prevent tearing.

Next, cut a piece of string 42 inches long. Guide one end of the string through the hole at the top of the kite, and tie it securely to the centerpole [1]. Take the other end of the string and loop it two or three times through a bridle ring (a curtain ring makes a fine bridle ring). Then guide the other end of the string through the hole at the bottom of the kite, and tie it securely to the centerpole [1]. Adjust the placement of the bridle ring by sliding it along the string until it is in a position directly above the center of the entire kite. When the bridle ring is properly adjusted, wrap a small piece of adhesive tape around the ring to hold the bridle strings secure. After test-flying the kite, you may have to adjust the bridle.

The final step in creating the butterfly kite is to attach tails [7] that will stabilize the kite in flight. Two 15-foot strips of crepe paper should be used for the tails. You can get some ideas for decorating these tails [7] by studying the full-color illustration of the Chinese Butterfly Kite. When the two tails [7] are ready, glue them to the two lowest sections of the kite frame.

The butterfly kite is now ready to fly. It will perform best in light to gentle winds.

The Chinese Butterfly Kite

Scale: Grid Squares = 1" (except as noted)

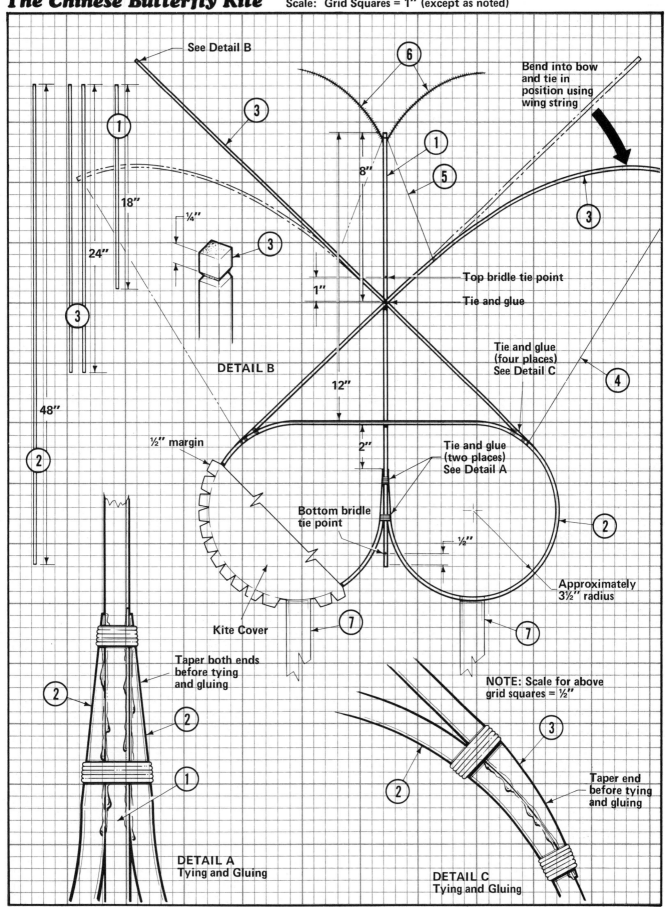

See Detail B

Bend into bow and tie in position using wing string

18"

24"

48"

¼"

DETAIL B

8"

1"

12"

2"

Top bridle tie point

Tie and glue

Tie and glue (four places) See Detail C

Tie and glue (two places) See Detail A

½" margin

Bottom bridle tie point

½"

Kite Cover

Approximately 3½" radius

NOTE: Scale for above grid squares = ½"

Taper both ends before tying and gluing

DETAIL A
Tying and Gluing

Taper end before tying and gluing

DETAIL C
Tying and Gluing

The Asian Fighting Kite

K ITE FIGHTING is a traditional and popular sport in many Asian countries. It is a war in the skies, complete with tactics and strategy, attack and defense. The object is to entangle the opponent's kite, causing it to lose lift or stability, or actually to sever the opponent's line, setting the kite free.

Fighting kites are specially built to damage and destroy other fighting kites in hotly contested combat. Razor blades or chips of glass encrusted in glue are attached to the kite line for the purpose of slashing through the opponent's kite or kite string. Tradition holds that the vanquished kite is the spoil that goes to the victor.

Fighting kites are constructed without tails. Controlled simply by their own balance and the skill of the kite-flyer, they dart and

Editor's Note: The numbers and detail citations that appear in brackets [ ] throughout this chapter refer to the scale drawing of The Asian Fighting Kite.

swoop quickly through the air. The directions for this fighting kite are based on the durable Japanese Nagasakihata kite which is as attractive as it is effective and exciting.

Kite Frame Materials

SPLIT CANE or bamboo is the best material to use for the frame of the fighting kite. It is strong and lightweight, and it has the additional advantage of being flexible enough to be bent into various shapes. You can purchase split bamboo at most craft and hobby stores, but you can also use the split bamboo from discarded outdoor or porch shades. If you decide to split your own bamboo from an old pole or cane, make certain that the resulting spars are no larger than a quarter of an inch square.

How To Create An Asian Fighting Kite

ONLY TWO SPARS are needed to construct the frame of this fighting kite. A 36-inch spar [1] serves as the centerpole, while a 43-inch spar [2] forms the bowed cross-spar. Build the fighting kite to the measurements given here because it may become unwieldy if you construct it any larger.

After you cut the two spars [1 and 2] to their proper size, you are ready for the single most important step in the construction of a successful fighting kite: you must prepare the long spar [2] so that it will bow properly. What you want is a spar that will bend into a symmetrical curve and fall into an even and springy although somewhat flattened arc.

First, use a sharp knife or sandpaper to smooth any bulges, blisters, or rough edges

on the spar. Next, carefully flex the cross-spar [2] and note any areas that need additional sanding to insure a symmetrical arc. When you are satisfied that the bow is properly prepared, take a sharp knife or saw and notch both ends of the cross-spar [2]. Now, notch both ends of the centerpole [1] as well [Detail A]. Later, you will secure the kite's string just below the notches [Detail A].

At this point, you must test the balance of both spars [1 and 2] by marking the exact center of each spar with a pencil line and then balancing the spar on the edge of a knife blade at its center mark. If one side of the spar tends to dip downward, correct the imbalance by whittling or sandpapering the heavier side until the spar balances properly.

Once both spars are balanced, it is time to join them together. The point of juncture should be made at the center of the cross-spar [2], nine inches down from the top of the centerpole [1]. Place the spars in the proper position, and then lash them together with common four-ply cotton string; the string should be strong without adding extra bulk. Wrap the string at least two turns through both diagonals created by the point of juncture, and then weave the string over and under the spars. Finally, tie it with a square knot, and trim off any excess string.

You are now ready to add the guideline string [3]. As you attach the guideline string [3], the cross-spar [2] will bow downward until both ends are level with the center of the centerpole [1]. Attach the guideline string [3] to the right-hand side of the cross-spar [2] by knotting it securely. Next, run the guideline string [3] to the notch at the bottom of the cen-

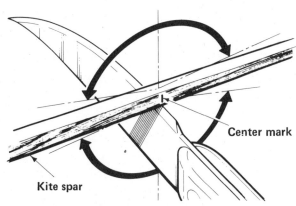

Balance the spar on a knife blade's edge.

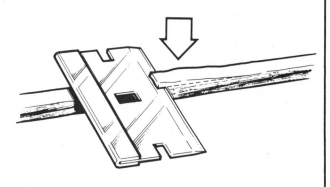

Trim the spar's heavier side until it balances properly.

Center mark

Kite spar

terpole [1], pulling the string taut as you do [Detail A]. When the cross-spar [2] bows to its proper position, lash the guideline string [3] securely to the bottom of the centerpole [1]. Continue running the guideline string [3] on to the left-hand side of the cross-spar [2], bowing it in place. Then tie the guideline string [3] securely to this end of the cross-spar [2]. Continue running the guideline string [3] on around the frame, always keeping it taut and making the knots secure, until the kite is completely framed. Then tie the two ends of the guideline string [3] together, allowing no slack as you do so.

Now test the entire kite frame for balance. Successful flying and effective maneuvering in flight depend on the kite frame being balanced precisely on either side of the centerpole [1]. In order to test the balance, place one end of the centerpole [1] on the tip of your finger. The frame should rest along a horizontal plane. If the frame tends to dip to one side, the imbalance must be corrected before you proceed any further in the construction. Measure to be sure that the cross-spar [2] is exactly centered over the centerpole [1]. Check then to see that both sides bow equally. If you spot either of these faults, adjust the string until the cross-spar [2] is properly positioned and bowed. If the imbalance persists, the cause will probably be found in the unequal weight of the sides of the cross-spar [2]. To correct such a problem, pare or sandpaper the heavier side until the kite balances properly.

When you are satisfied that the frame is

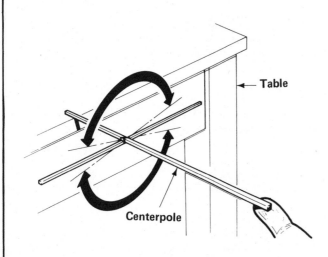

Test the entire kite frame for balance.

balanced, apply glue to the string knots at the center joint and at the ends of the spars. Use a quick-drying glue that becomes tough rather than brittle, and be sure to use enough glue to soak the string of the knots and joints thoroughly. Now set the kite frame aside and allow it to dry.

Preparing The Kite Cover

YOU ARE NOW ready to prepare the covering for the fighting kite. Paper is the most popular cover material for the fighting kite, but remember that the paper must be both strong and lightweight. You can use anything from wrapping paper to tissue paper, newspaper, rice paper, or the type of imitation Japanese paper found in art supply stores.

Place the kite frame on the kite covering, and then trace around the outside edge of the frame (the guideline string [3]) with a pencil, leaving a half-inch margin around the entire kite. Later, you will glue this margin around the string frame. Now cut notches in the margin at the four points where the spars should protrude.

After tracing the frame pattern on the kite cover, use sharp scissors to cut the cover to size.

It is time to decorate the kite cover. Refer to the chapter "Decorating The Kite" and to the full-color illustration of the Asian Fighting Kite for ideas.

Now position the kite frame over the undecorated side of the kite covering with the cross-spar [2] against the covering and the centerpole [1] above it. Crease the half-inch margin of the kite cover over the string frame to provide a guideline, and apply glue to the margin. Then seal the margin securely with the string inside. Work slowly to avoid any wrinkles or creases, and wait until the glue is completely dry before proceeding to the next step.

The next step involves creation of a two-legged bridle, which is necessary to control the angle at which the surface of the kite meets the wind. First, cut a piece of string 82 inches long [4]. Now, using a nail or a sharp-pointed tool, carefully make a hole in the kite cover directly over the point of juncture of the centerpole [1] and the bowed cross-spar [2]. Punch another hole over the centerpole [1] two inches from the bottom, and apply a notebook reinforcer to each hole to prevent tearing.

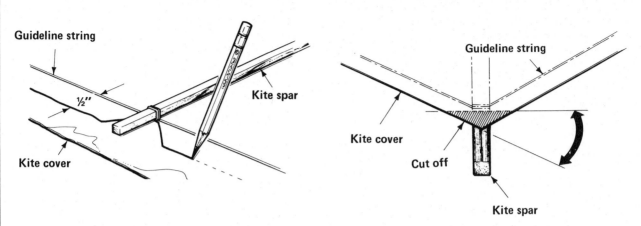

(LEFT) Trace around the guideline string, leaving a half-inch margin around the entire kite. (RIGHT) Cut notches in the margin at the four points where the spars will protrude.

Now guide one end of the bridle string [4] through the top hole and knot it securely to the frame. Then loop the bridle string [4] two or three times through a bridle ring (use a curtain ring for this purpose) at a position about three feet down the bridle string [4]. Guide the other end of the bridle string [4] through the hole at the bottom of the kite, and lash it securely to the centerpole [1]. When you have the bridle ring positioned properly, wrap a small piece of adhesive tape around it to hold the bridle string [4] secure.

Many people who make fighting kites often attach paper tassels to the ends of the cross-spar [2]. If you do likewise, be sure the tassels are equal in weight so as not to affect the kite's balance adversely [Detail B].

In addition to paper tassels, people who take kite fighting seriously fasten cutting weapons — broken glass, razor blades, and other lightweight but lethal objects — to the kites towing line. The cutting weapons should be embedded in glue to hold them secure [Detail C].

This fighting kite flies well in gentle to moderate winds, but you must experiment with and practice your flying technique before partaking in actual kite combat. When you feel confident of your own ability, though, you will have an excellent fighter to take into battle.

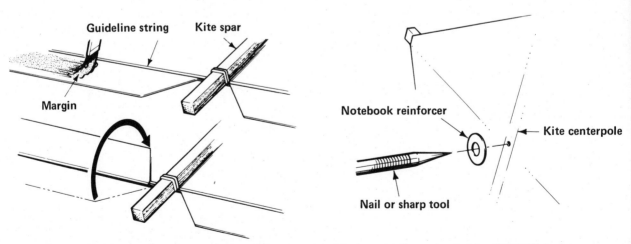

(LEFT) Apply glue to the margin and seal the margin securely with the guideline string inside. (RIGHT) Punch holes in the kite cover for the bridle string.

The Asian Fighting Kite Scale: Grid Squares = 1"

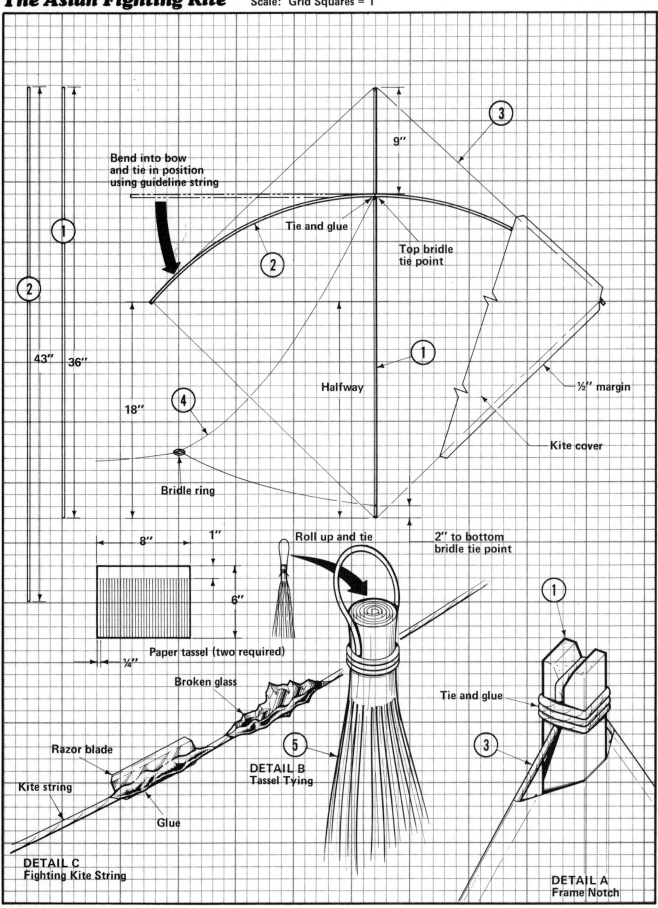

Bend into bow and tie in position using guideline string

Tie and glue

Top bridle tie point

9"

½" margin

Kite cover

Halfway

43" 36"

18"

Bridle ring

Roll up and tie

2" to bottom bridle tie point

8" 1"

6"

¼"

Paper tassel (two required)

Broken glass

Razor blade

Kite string

Glue

DETAIL C
Fighting Kite String

DETAIL B
Tassel Tying

Tie and glue

DETAIL A
Frame Notch

The Centipede Kite

A CENTIPEDE is an insect that is alleged to have 100 legs. It does not. Neither does the centipede kite, but even so it is one of the most unique and dazzling of all kites.

Creating the centipede kite is not a project for the beginning kite-maker. It is not only difficult to construct, but it is also difficult to fly. Once in flight, though, the centipede kite presents a spectacular sight as it shimmers and wiggles through the sky like no other kite you can make.

The centipede kite consists of a series of circular kite panels strung together. The first circle, the head of the centipede, is the largest circle; each of the following circular panels, which form the body, decreases in size from

Editor's Note: The numbers and detail citations that appear in brackets [ ] throughout this chapter refer to the scale drawing of The Centipede Kite.

the head to the tail. Depending on the number of circles used, the centipede kite can range from just a few feet to over 50 feet long. You must remember, however, that the longer the kite, the more difficult it is to fly. The directions given here are for a centipede kite comprising 10 circular panels.

Kite Frame Materials

THE FRAME of the centipede kite should be made from bamboo. In addition to the fact that it is strong and lightweight, bamboo is sufficiently flexible so that you can form it into circles. You can purchase split bamboo at most craft or hobby shops, but you may find just what you want — bamboo that is already split — in discarded outdoor porch shades. You can also split your own bamboo from an old bamboo cane or pole.

How To Create A Centipede Kite

YOU WILL NEED one spar to form the circle and two spars to provide the supporting frame for each panel of the centipede kite. Each bamboo spar should measure no larger than one-quarter of an inch square. For the head of the centipede kite — the largest circle — you will need a circular spar [1] 50 inches long and two 22-inch support spars [11]. Each succeeding circle requires a circular spar [2 through 10] that decreases in length by three inches and two supporting spars [12 through 20] that decrease in length by one inch. Therefore, to create the nine additional circles for the centipede kite, you will need the following:

Circular Spars (One in each size)	Support Spars (Two in each size)
47 inches [2]	21 inches [12]
44 inches [3]	20 inches [13]
41 inches [4]	19 inches [14]
38 inches [5]	18 inches [15]
35 inches [6]	17 inches [16]
32 inches [7]	16 inches [17]
29 inches [8]	15 inches [18]
26 inches [9]	14 inches [19]
23 inches [10]	13 inches [20]

When you finish cutting all the spars to their proper lengths, you must test for balance the two spars that will form each circle's supporting members. An essential element in successful kite-making, balance testing is accomplished by making a pencil line at the exact center of each spar and then balancing the spar at this point on the edge of a knife blade. If one side tends to dip downward, the spar is not balanced. You can correct any imbalance easily by whittling or sandpapering the heavier side until proper balance is achieved.

When you are satisfied that each of the support spars [11 through 20] is balanced, you are ready to join these spars together to construct the 10 support spar frames. Place the first support spar [11] on a flat surface. Position the second support spar [11] over the first at a 90-degree angle to form an "X." The support spars [11] must intersect at their exact centers, and the four angles formed by the criss-crossed support spars [11] must be exactly the same [Detail B].

When you have the support spars [11] correctly positioned, lash the point of the juncture with string. Use string that is strong

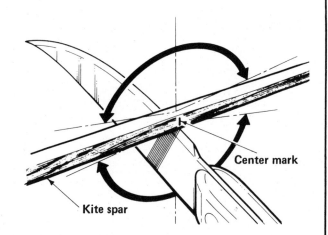

Balance the spar on the edge of a knife.

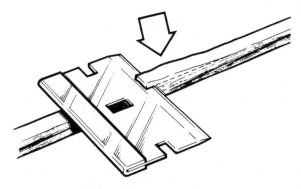

Trim down the spar's heavier side so that it balances.

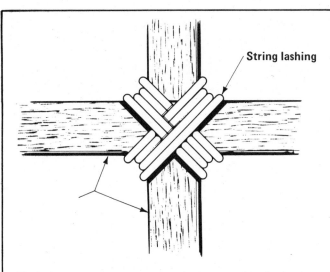

String lashing

To lash support spars, weave string over and under both diagonals at the point of juncture.

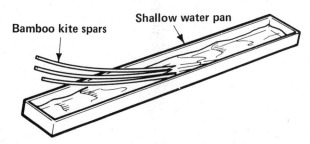

After lashing, tie the ends of the string into a square knot.

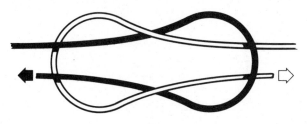

Bamboo kite spars   Shallow water pan

Soak spars in water for two hours to make them flexible.

Bamboo kite spar

Move the spar back and forth over a candle flame while bending it in the desired direction.

and that will not stretch or add unnecessary bulk; a common four-ply cotton string is suitable. To lash the support spars [11] in position, make at least two turns through both diagonals, and then weave the string over and under the support spars [11]. Finally, tie a square knot, and clip off any excess string. Repeat the same process for each of the other nine support frames.

The longer spars [1 through 10] which form the circles must be bent into the proper shape. Before preparing the bamboo for shaping, check to be sure that the spars bend evenly along their full length and that they are relatively free of irregularities like bumps and ridges which could adversely affect the kite's balance.

You can prepare the bamboo for shaping in either of two ways. One way is to soak the 10 bamboo circular spars [1 through 10] in water for approximately two hours or until they are flexible enough to bend easily without breaking. The other way employs heat to soften and shape the bamboo. In this alternative method, you move each circular bamboo spar back and forth over a candle flame while simultaneously applying gentle pressure to bend the spar in the direction desired. Be careful, however, not to hold the bamboo motionless over the flame because you can burn it or permanently deform it and thereby make it useless as a circular spar frame.

When the bamboo is satisfactorily flexible, you are ready to form the circular frames. To begin, take the first circular spar [1] and notch each end of it to facilitate lashing [Detail A]. Now overlap the notched ends to form the desired circle. Apply glue to the joint, or point of overlap, to bind the circular spar frame. Any glue that dries quickly and that does not become brittle is suitable for this job. Now lash the joint with string. When tying two surfaces that run parallel, it is best to make two lashings as far apart as possible [Detail A]. Secure the lashing with a square knot or tie the knot twice on each lashing.

The next step is to lash the circular spar frame [1] to each of the four points of the "X" created by the support spar frame [11]. It is very important that the circular spar frame [1] be perfectly centered on the support spar frame [11]; therefore, measure to be sure that the support spars [11] extend equally beyond the circular spar frame [1] at all four points.

When you are satisfied that the circular

spar frame [1] is properly positioned, lash it to the support spar frame [11] at each of the four points of juncture [Detail B]. Be sure to take at least two turns through both diagonals of the point of intersection; then weave the string over and under the spars and tie it with a square knot. Clip off any excess string. Repeat the same process for each of the remaining nine circular frames.

Since it is crucial that each frame balance precisely on either side of the supporting spars [11], you must test both of the perpendicular support spars in the following manner. Place one end of a support spar [11] on the tip of your finger and rest the other end on the edge of a table. The kite frame should lay along a horizontal plane. If the frame tends to dip to one side, it is not balanced.

To correct any imbalance, measure to be sure that the support spars [11] are centered and that they extend out equally from the circular spar frame [1] at all four points. Make any necessary adjustments. If this does not correct the imbalance, the cause probably lies in an unequal weight of the spars themselves. Whittle or sandpaper the heavier side of the spar in question until total balance is achieved. Then rotate the circular spar frame [1] and test the other support spar [11] for balance in the same fashion. All 10 frames must be checked for balance before proceeding in the construction of the centipede kite.

When you are satisfied that all the frames are in balance, you are ready to apply glue to the lashings of each frame. Be sure to use enough glue to soak the string of the joints and knots thoroughly. Now set the frames aside and allow them to dry completely.

Preparing The Kite Cover

YOU ARE NOW ready to prepare the coverings for the 10 panels of the centipede kite. The cover material most commonly used for this kite is paper; but the paper must be both strong and lightweight. Suitable types include wrapping paper, tissue paper, newspaper, shelf paper, brown paper, rice paper, or imitation Japanese paper like that normally found in art supply stores.

Place the first circular spar frame [1] on top of the kite cover material. With a pencil, trace around the outside edge of the circular spar frame [1], leaving a half-inch margin all the way around. The margin provides the over-

lap which you will later glue around the frame. Once you have traced the shape properly on the kite cover, cut along the pencil line carefully and evenly with sharp scissors. Finally, notch or scallop the margin to allow for smooth folding [Detail B]. Prepare the kite covers for the other nine panels in the same way.

With the coverings cut to size, it is time to decorate the kite cover. Refer to the chapter "Decorating The Kite" and to the full-color illustration of the Centipede Kite for ideas.

After you finish decorating the kite (wait until the kite cover is thoroughly dry), position one of the circular spar frames on top of the undecorated side of its appropriate kite cover. Then crease and glue the margin over the frame. Work slowly and carefully to avoid wrinkles and creases. When the margin is sealed securely over the frame, put the panel aside until the glue is thoroughly dry.

When all 10 panels have been covered and the glue has dried, it is time to join the panels together to form the centipede. Join the panels together in three places : (1) over the joint formed by the circular spar frame and the top of the vertical support spar; (2) over the joint formed by the circular spar frame and one side of the horizontal support spar; and, (3) over the joint formed by the circular spar frame and the other side of the horizontal support spar.

Now, with a nail or other pointed tool carefully punch a hole through the kite cover at each of these three positions on each of the 10 panels, and apply a notebook reinforcer to each hole to prevent tearing. Then, cut three pieces of string, each 15 inches long. These pieces of string must be very strong because they will be subject to the tremendous pull exerted on the panels when the kite is in flight.

Guide the end of one piece of string through the hole at the top of the next largest panel and tie it securely to the frame, leaving 12 inches of string between the head panel and the second panel. Next, tie the second piece of string in the same manner, taking it through the holes at the right side of the head panel and the second panel; secure it by tying it in the same way as you did the first piece of string. Again, there should be 12 inches of string between the two panels. Repeat the same process with the third piece of string, guiding it through the holes on the left side of the head panel and the second panel and tying each end securely.

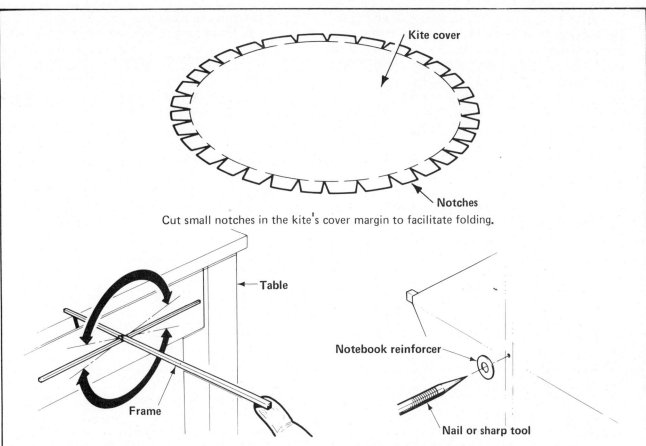

Cut small notches in the kite's cover margin to facilitate folding.

Kite cover

Notches

Table

Frame

Notebook reinforcer

Nail or sharp tool

(LEFT) Test the kite frame for balance by resting one end of the support spar on the tip of your finger and the other end on the edge of a table. (RIGHT) Punch holes in the kite cover with a nail or sharp tool for the bridle string.

Join each additional kite panel to the one ahead of it in the same manner, but decrease the distance between each succeeding panel by one-half inch [Detail C]. The string between the second and third panels, therefore, will be 11½ inches long, 11 inches between the third and fourth panels, and so forth. All the panels are parallel to each other, and, of course, they follow one another in decreasing size.

Once you have lashed all the panels together, prepare a two-legged bridle for the kite. Use a nail or other pointed object to punch a hole just inside the joint formed by the bottom of the circular spar frame [1] and the vertical support spar [11] of the head panel. Apply a notebook reinforcer around the hole. Now, cut a piece of strong string 36 inches long [21]. Guide one end of the string through the hole at the top of the head panel and tie it securely to the frame. Thread the other end of the string [21] two or three times through a bridle ring; a curtain ring makes a fine bridle ring. Then guide the other end of the string

[21] through the hole you just punched at the bottom of the kite and tie it securely to the frame.

You can adjust the placement of the bridle ring by sliding it along the string until it is in position directly above the center of the kite's head panel. When the bridle ring is properly adjusted, wrap a small piece of adhesive tape around the ring to hold the bridle strings secure.

To complete the centipede kite, glue two long (4-inch x 60-inch) paper tails [22] to the last panel [10]. Then decorate your centipede kite with paper tassels or streamers attached to both ends of the horizontal support spar on each panel of the kite.

The centipede kite is not a high-flying kite, but it produces one of the most sensational sights in the sky as it loops and quivers in its own unique form of flight. To get the centipede kite off the ground and keep it flying, however, you will need a helper and at least moderate wind velocity.

The Centipede Kite

Scale: Grid Squares = 1"

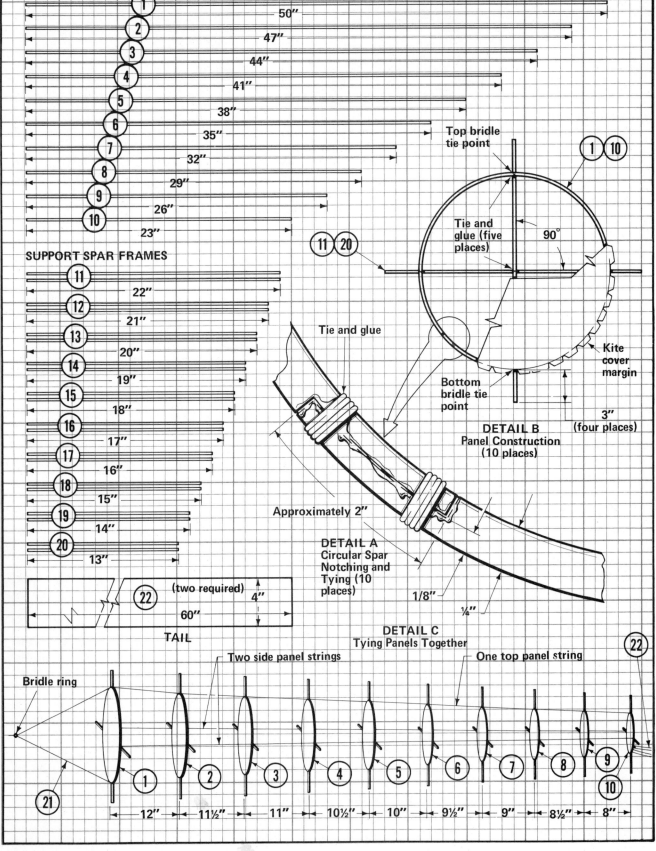

CIRCULAR SPAR FRAMES

1 — 50"
2 — 47"
3 — 44"
4 — 41"
5 — 38"
6 — 35"
7 — 32"
8 — 29"
9 — 26"
10 — 23"

SUPPORT SPAR FRAMES

11 — 22"
12 — 21"
13 — 20"
14 — 19"
15 — 18"
16 — 17"
17 — 16"
18 — 15"
19 — 14"
20 — 13"

22 (two required) 4"
60"

TAIL

Top bridle tie point

1 10

Tie and glue (five places)

90°

11 20

Kite cover margin

3" (four places)

Bottom bridle tie point

DETAIL B
Panel Construction
(10 places)

Tie and glue

Approximately 2"

DETAIL A
Circular Spar
Notching and
Tying (10 places)

1/8"

¼"

DETAIL C
Tying Panels Together

Two side panel strings

One top panel string

Bridle ring

21

1 2 3 4 5 6 7 8 9 10

22

12" 11½" 11" 10½" 10" 9½" 9" 8½" 8"

The Elaborate Parafoil Kite

THE CREATION of the parafoil kite by aeronautical engineer Domina Jalbert introduced a new form of kite to the scene. The parafoil kite, which looks almost like an inflated mattress in flight, is a combination of an airfoil — that is, the shape of airplane wings — the inflation principles of a wind sock, and some of the characteristics of a parachute. The net result is a highly efficient kite with great lifting power.

The size of the parafoil kite is determined by the number of its inflatable cells. A large

parafoil is capable of transporting heavy loads or even carrying a human being aloft. The directions for this version result in a smaller but still elaborate parafoil kite.

A parafoil kite is constructed entirely of fabric, without any supporting spars. You must

> **Editor's Note:** The numbers and detail citations that appear in brackets [ ] throughout this chapter refer to the scale drawing of The Elaborate Parafoil Kite.

stitch the cells of the kite together with strong thread, since kite's support comes solely from the stitching and the hemmed edges.

The parafoil is a difficult kite to construct. Only those kite creators who are skilled at sewing should tackle this project. Measurements, moreover, must be absolutely precise; proportion is critical, and if the measurements given here are not followed closely, the kite may not fly satisfactorily.

To decorate this kite, you can follow the full-color illustration of the Elaborate Parafoil Kite or create your own design with your own choice of colored materials.

Kite Materials

THE FIRST STEP in constructing this parafoil kite is to select a proper material. The fabric must be lightweight and strong, but it must also be flexible. A Bainbridge cloth, like Zephyrlite or Stabilkote, is ideal. Lightweight ripstop spinmaker nylon can also be effective.

How To Create An Elaborate Parafoil Kite

ONCE YOU OBTAIN the proper material, your first step is to cut out the sections that will form the top and the bottom panels of the kite. For the top panels [1], cut two rectangular pieces of kite material 36 inches long and 14 inches wide. The two pieces should be taken from fabric of different colors. Mark the fabric, using a ruler or straightedge, to be sure your lines are straight. Next, divide each piece along its width into two equal sections, each seven inches by 36 inches. Cut out each of these panels which will form the kite's top covering.

For the bottom panels [2] cut two differently colored rectangles of material 14 inches by 33 inches. Again divide each rectangle into two panels so that you have four pieces, each seven inches by 33 inches, and cut out the panels with sharp scissors.

You must now prepare the airfoil shape [3] that will be sewn between the top and bottom sections. It is helpful to first make a paper pattern of the five airfoils [3] needed here. Later, this pattern will serve as the guide from which you can cut the actual kite material.

To prepare the airfoil [3] pattern, first draw a straight horizontal line 33 inches long. Then mark nine dots to form the outline of the airfoil. To mark each of these dots correctly, measure up from the baseline in the following manner:

1. Five inches in from the left end of the baseline and two inches up.
2. Nine inches in from the left end of the baseline and three inches up.
3. Thirteen inches in from the left end of the baseline and four inches up.
4. Seventeen inches in from the left end of the baseline and 4¾ inches up.
5. Twenty-one inches in from the left end of the baseline and 5¼ inches up.
6. Twenty-five inches in from the left end of the baseline and 5½ inches up.
7. Twenty-nine inches in from the left end of the baseline and five inches up.
8. Thirty-three inches in from the left end of the baseline and four inches up.
9. Thirty-five inches in from the left end of the baseline and three inches up.

Now, draw a gently curving line from the left end of the 33-inch horizontal baseline through the dots. Then draw a straight line from the right end of the baseline to the right end of the curving line. You have now created the airfoil shape. Cut it out and use the paper pattern as a guide for cutting out the five airfoils [3] from the kite cover material. Make sure that your scissors are sharp to insure a neat, trim cutting line.

The final sections to be cut are the ventral fins [4]. Again you will find it helpful to make a paper pattern. To draw the rear ventral fin pattern [4], start with a horizontal line 21 inches long. Mark a dot at a position 13½ inches above the left end of the horizontal line. Now, using a ruler or straightedge, draw a line connecting this dot with the left end of the horizontal line. To complete the pattern, draw another line from the dot to the right end of the horizontal line. Then cut three separate rear ventral fins [4] from the kite cover material, using this pattern as a guide for all three.

Now you are ready to prepare the pattern for the front ventral fins [5]. Draw a horizontal line 15 inches long. Mark a dot at a position that is 10 inches below and four inches to the left of the right end of the horizontal line. Draw a straight line connecting this dot to the right end of the horizontal line. Then draw another straight line from the dot to the left end of the horizontal line. Now cut three front ventral fins [5] from the kite cover materials.

Next comes the process of joining the panels, airfoils, and ventral fins together. You must stitch them carefully with strong thread. In addition, you must tie the thread ends securely because the wind will place a great deal of pressure on all the sewed areas, and any unraveling will quickly lead to the destruction of the kite. For this reason, it is best to hem all the edges of all the pieces before actually joining the panels, airfoils, and ventral fins together to form the kite.

The first step in stitching the panels together is to sew the front [5] and rear [4] ventral fins onto the bottom edge of three airfoils [3]. Place one airfoil [3] so that its 33-inch edge overlaps the 21-inch edge of one of the rear ventral fins [4]. Carefully stitch along this line, and knot the end of the thread securely. Next, place a front ventral fin [5] in front of the rear ventral fin [4] so that its 15-inch edge overlaps the 33-inch edge of the airfoil [3]. Now carefully stitch along this line. Notice that the ventral fins overlap one another; do not sew this overlap together. Attach the front and rear ventral fins [4 and 5] to two more airfoils [3] in the same manner as you did the first one.

You are now ready to join the airfoil [3] to the four bottom panels [2]. Place either 33-inch bottom panel [2] on a flat surface. If you did not hem this panel, crease a ¼-inch fold along its long edge. Now place one of the airfoils [3] to which front and rear ventral fins [4 and 5] have been attached alongside the crease in the bottom panel [2], and stitch the airfoil [3] and the bottom panel [2] together. All hems and stitched edges should be on the inside when the kite construction is finished.

Next, working slowly and carefully to keep the fabric smooth, join the other side of the 33-inch bottom panel [2] to the bottom edge of an airfoil [3] without front and rear ventral fins [4 and 5]. Again, be sure to crease ¼-inch of the panel edge if you did not hem, and be sure that all sewn edges will end up inside the parafoil. Now join another bottom panel [2] — this one of the other color material — by stitching along the same line.

The next airfoil to be joined, the one in the center of the kite, must be one with front and rear ventral fins [4 and 5] attached. You must stitch it to the other side of the second bottom panel [2] in the same manner as before. When this is done, join another bottom panel [2] — the same color as the first — along the same seam line. Then stitch an airfoil [3] without front and rear ventral fins [4 and 5] to the other

side of this bottom panel [2]. Attach the last bottom panel [2] along the same seam line, and, finally, stitch the last airfoil [3] with front and rear ventral fins to the edge of the last bottom panel [2].

The next step in sewing the kite together involves joining the top panels [1] to the tops of the airfoils [3]. Make the first top panel [1] one that is the opposite color of the first bottom panel [2]. Work slowly, keeping the sewn edge inside as you work from cell to cell.

With all four cells of your kite complete, the final step in sewing the parafoil together is to stitch the top [1] and bottom [2] panels together about two inches from the back of the kite.

To complete the kite, you must now add the shroud lines. First, reinforce the six tips of the front and rear ventral fins by sewing triangular pieces of cloth, cut from scrap material, to match the tips of the front and rear ventral fins [4 and 5]. Then make a sturdy buttonhole in the reinforced tip [Detail A].

Now cut three pieces of cord or fishing line to lengths of 56 inches each. The line must be about 80-pound test strength because great tension will be exerted on the line in flight. Guide the end of one cord through the hole in a front ventral fin [5] and lash it securely. Loop the other end of the cord two or three times through a bridle ring (a curtain ring will suffice), and position the bridle ring about midway on the length of cord. Then guide the end through the hole of the corresponding rear ventral fin [4] and tie it securely. Attach the other two shroud lines in the same way.

Attach a single tail — to promote lateral stability — approximately 60 inches long and four inches wide at the center of the kite's back edge. Commercially manufactured parafoil kites often use a drogue type of tail. This resembles an open bucket, 10 or 12 inches tall, which you can make from scraps of cover material. Attach the drogue to a six-foot single tail or to a drogue line.

The parafoil kite is an interesting kite to fly. Its take-off is quite steep, and you will feel a great deal of pull as it soars almost directly overhead. The parafoil kite has an advantage in that it can fly in any breeze strong enough to inflate it; it is, in fact, among the best kites in terms of having a wide range of suitable wind conditions for launching and flying. A unique kite to observe, the parafoil is certainly an exciting one to fly.

Elaborate Parafoil   Scale: Grid Squares = 1"

TOP PANELS (white)   36"   14"   7"   ①   ①

Cut along dotted line (four places)

TOP PANELS (orange)   14"   7"   ①   ①

BOTTOM PANELS (white)   14"   7"   ②   ②

BOTTOM PANELS (orange)   14"   7"   ②   ②   33"

AIRFOIL PATTERN (orange) (five required)   ③

3"   2"   4"   5"   5½"   5¼"   4¾"   4"   3"   2"   4" (seven places)   33"   5"

TAIL (white)   60"   4"   ⑥

FRONT VENTRAL FIN (yellow) (three required)   ⑤   15"   10"   4"   Bridle tie corner

REAR VENTRAL FIN (yellow) (three required)   ④   21"   13½"   Bridle tie corner

104

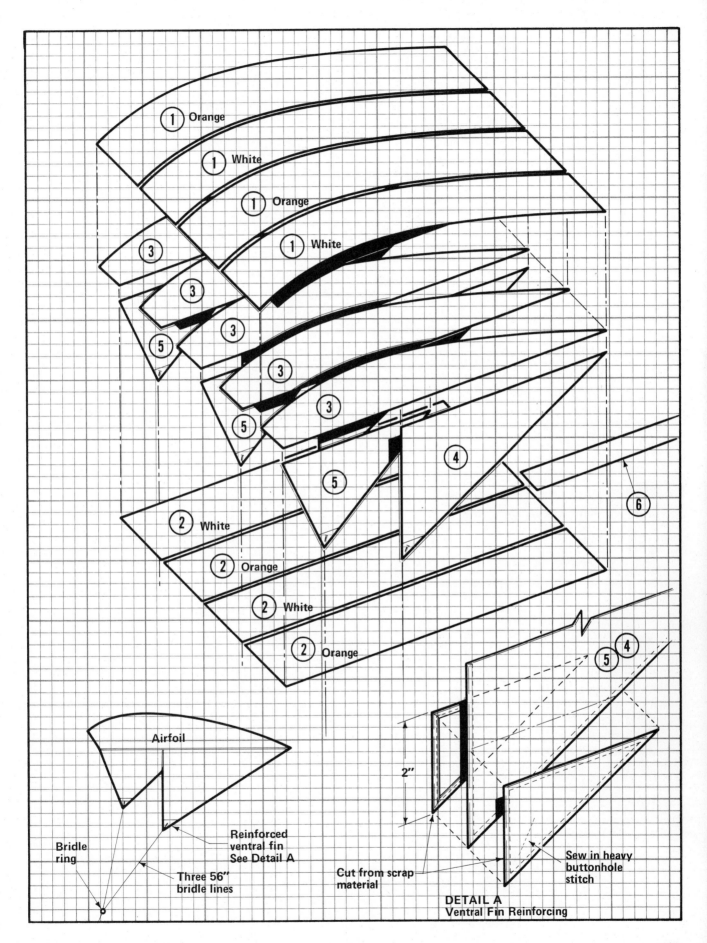

① Orange

① White

① Orange

③

③

① White

③

⑤

③

⑤

③

④

⑤

② White

⑥

② Orange

② White

⑤ ④

② Orange

Airfoil

2″

Bridle
ring

Reinforced
ventral fin
See Detail A

Three 56″
bridle lines

Cut from scrap
material

Sew in heavy
buttonhole
stitch

DETAIL A
Ventral Fin Reinforcing

The Chinese Fertility Kite

THE CHINESE fertility kite (or Chinese rice kite, as it is sometimes called) was originally a ritual kite, flown in China in conjunction with a prayer for a good rice crop. The kite frame was equipped with sheaves of freshly picked rice attached at each corner and at the tail. As the kite was flown above the rice paddies, grains of rice would be shaken loose from the sheaves and scattered over the ground in a symbolic reproduction of the fertilization process. Asians still fly this kite, although they do it more for tradition than as a part of a religious ritual.

The flat kite design is the most popular one for fertility kites. And thus, with or without the attachment of rice sheaves, fertility kites are at their best flying in moderate winds.

Kite Frame Materials

SPLIT BAMBOO is the material to use for the fertility kite frame. Strong but lightweight, split bamboo can be bent rather easily, and it will retain its bent shape. You can purchase split bamboo at many craft stores and hobby shops, but you may find just what you need in discarded outdoor porch shades made of split bamboo. You can, of course, split your own bamboo from an old bamboo pole or cane.

Editor's Note: The numbers and detail citations that appear in brackets [ ] throughout this chapter refer to the scale drawing of The Chinese Fertility Kite.

Just make sure that the bamboo spars you use for the fertility kite are no larger than a quarter-inch square.

How To Create A Chinese Fertility Kite

YOU WILL NEED seven spars to construct the frame for this kite. A 42-inch spar [1] will form the centerpole of the kite; two 36-inch spars [2] will form the topmost oval; two 28-inch spars [3] will form the middle oval; and two 18-inch spars [4] are needed for the bottom oval.

Test each of the spars for balance. You do this by marking the center of each spar and then placing the spar at its center point on the edge of a knife blade. If one side tends to go down, the spar is not balanced. You can correct this imbalance easily by whittling or sandpapering the heavier side until the spar balances on the knife blade. Good balance is an absolute requirement for successful kite-making.

When you are satisfied that all the spars are balanced, soak the six shorter spars [2,3, and 4] — the ones that will form the kite's three oval panels — in water for several hours. After soaking the spars in water, you will be able to bend them without their splitting or cracking.

When the spars are sufficiently flexible, you are ready to begin constructing the kite frame. First, cut 16 pieces of string, each to a length of eight inches; these will be used to lash the joints of the kite frame together. The string should be strong and it should not stretch, but it should not be so heavy that it adds bulk to the kite frame. A common four-ply cotton string is quite suitable for lashing.

Place one of the 36-inch spars [2] on a flat surface, and position the second 36-inch spar [2] so that its end is perpendicular to the first spar [2] at the point of overlap; the overlap should form an approximate 90-degree angle [Detail A]. Now, at the point of juncture, lash the two spars [2] together with one of the eight-inch lengths of string. Make at least two turns with the lashing through both diagonals of the crossing point. Then weave the string over and under the spars [2] and tie the ends into a square knot. Clip off any excess string.

After securing the juncture of the spars [2] at one end, cross them at the opposite end so that both spars [2] are bowed into an oval, and so that the overlapping ends form an approximate 90-degree angle. Then tie the spars [2]

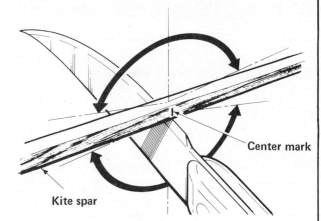

Balance the spar on the edge of a knife.

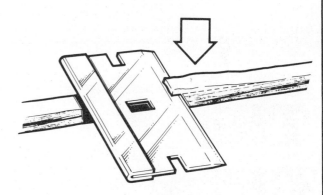

Trim off any bumps or irregularities.

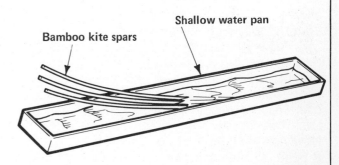

Bamboo kite spars   Shallow water pan

Soak the spars in water before bending them.

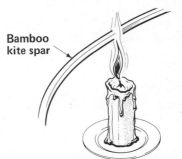

Bamboo kite spar

Passing the bamboo spar back and forth over a candle flame will make the spar flexible for bending.

here just as you did at the opposite end.

Now take the two 28-inch spars [3] and construct another oval shape in exactly the same way. Repeat the process with the two 18-inch spars [4]. You now have constructed the three oval panels of the kite frame.

It is time to attach the three ovals [2,3, and 4] to the centerpole [1]. Place the 42-inch centerpole [1] on a flat surface, and position the largest oval [2] four inches below its top. The center marks of each spar [2] of the oval must be directly over the centerpole [1]. Now lash the top of the oval [2] to the centerpole [1] with one of the eight-inch lengths of string [Detail B], following the same procedure described for lashing the ends of the spars. Check the position of the lower spar [2] of the oval to be sure it is directly over the centerpole [1], and then lash it to the centerpole [1] in the same fashion. The lower spar [2] should be lashed at a point 20 inches down from the top of the centerpole [1].

Now place the middle-sized oval [3] over the centerpole [1] so that the top of this oval is 16 inches down from the top of the centerpole [1]. This means that the middle-sized oval [3] overlaps the larger oval [2]. Make certain that the center marks of each spar [3] rest directly on the centerpole [1]. Now lash both the top and bottom spars [3] of this oval to the centerpole [1], using the same lashing techniques as before. The bottom spar of this oval [3] should be lashed at a point 28 inches down from the top of the centerpole [1].

Position the last and smallest oval [4] over the centerpole [1] so that the top of this oval [4] is 26 inches down from the top of the centerpole [1]. Thus, the smallest oval [4] overlaps the middle-sized oval [3] above it. Lash the top spar [4] to the centerpole [1]. Now lash the bottom of the smallest oval [4] at a point 35 inches down from the top of the centerpole [1]. Before tying them, however, check to be certain that the center mark of each spar [4] is directly over the centerpole [1]. There should be seven inches of centerpole [1] extending downward from the third oval [4].

You must now tie the curved sections together at the four points where they intersect [Detail C]. Before tying them, however, measure to be sure that the points of intersection are exactly equidistant from the centerpole [1]; this is important to insure proper balance for the kite.

After lashing, tie the strings into a square knot.

At this point, you must test the entire kite frame for balance. It is crucial that the frame balance precisely on either side of the centerpole. In order to test the frame for balance, lay one end of the centerpole [1] on a table and place the other end on the tip of your finger, balancing the frame on a horizontal plane. If it remains in this position, the frame is in balance. If the frame tends to dip to one side, however, it is not properly balanced, and you must correct the imbalance before proceeding any further. To do so, first take measurements to ascertain that the center of each spar is positioned directly over the centerpole [1]; make any necessary adjustments. If the positioning of the ovals is correct, then the cause of the imbalance will undoubtedly be found in the unequal weight of the spars on one side of the centerpole [1]. In that case, shave or sandpaper the heavier side of the spar until the frame balances properly.

When you are satisfied that the frame is in balance, apply glue to the lashings. Any glue that dries quickly and becomes tough rather than brittle is appropriate for this job. Be sure, however, that you use enough glue to soak the string of the joints and knots thoroughly. Now set the frame aside until the glue is completely dry, at which time you will have a sturdy frame on which to build the fertility kite.

Preparing The Kite Cover

THE NEXT STEP is to prepare the covering for the kite panels. Since the cover must be

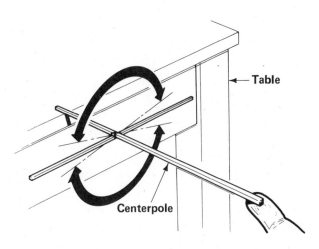

Test the entire kite frame for balance.

both lightweight and strong, paper is the most common material used, but remember that the wind must not be able to blow through the kite cover. Any strong and durable paper — e.g., newspaper, shelf paper, wrapping paper, tissue paper, brown paper, rice paper, or imitation Japanese paper — will work very nicely.

You must cut three separate sections to cover the panels of the fertility kite frame. The two overlapping areas between the panels, however, are to be left open.

Begin by placing the kite frame on the kite cover, with the frame's centerpole [1] away

from the covering. Use a pencil to trace an outline around the outside edge of each panel, allowing a one-inch margin around each panel. Later, you will wrap and glue this margin around the frame itself. Be sure to adjust your marking in order to maintain the one-inch margin at the points of overlap.

Once you finish tracing the patterns of the panels onto the covering, cut them out. You will find it helpful later on in folding the covering around the kite frame if you cut little notches in the one-inch margin.

With the covering cut to size, it is time to

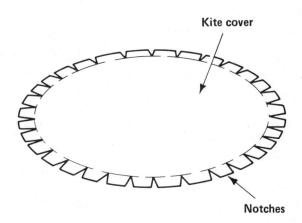

To facilitate folding the kite cover around the kite frame, cut little notches in the one-inch margin.

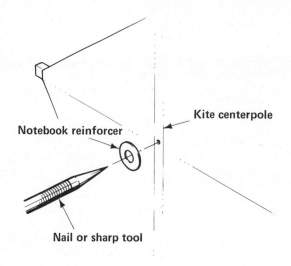

Notebook reinforcer

Kite centerpole

Nail or sharp tool

Punch holes in the cover for the bridle string.

decorate. You can use paints (watercolors, poster paints, or water-thinned acrylic colors), crayons, or ink. Whatever kind of paint you use, though, should be a type that will dry quickly and that is both flexible and lightweight when dry. Do not proceed with kite construction until you are sure that the paint is completely dry. Refer to the chapter "Decorating The Kite" and to the full-color illustration of the Chinese Fertility Kite for ideas.

The next step involves gluing the kite covers to the frame panels. First, crease the margin over the frame to provide a guideline. Then apply glue to the margin and seal it securely around the frame itself.

After you glue the cover around the frame — and the glue has dried thoroughly — you must prepare a bridle to control the angle at which the surface of the kite meets the wind. With a nail or other pointed tool, carefully punch a hole in the kite cover at the center of the top oval panel [2], directly over the centerpole [1]. Apply a notebook reinforcer around the hole to prevent tearing. Now cut a piece of string 92 inches long, and guide one end of the string through the hole, tying it securely to the centerpole [1] of the kite. Then take the other end of the string and loop it two or three times through a bridle ring; a curtain ring makes a good bridle ring. Position the bridle ring about 50 inches from the untied end of the string, and then tie this end of the string to

the centerpole [1] one inch below the bottom oval [4]. Do not trim the excess string after tying the bridle; you may need it later for adjusting the bridle after test-flying the kite.

The final procedure is to prepare a tail [5] for the fertility kite. Like all flat kites, it must have a tail to provide stabilization during flight. The fertility kite can have a tail made entirely of rice sheaves, or it can have a paper streamer or other conventional tail to which a rice sheaf can be attached. If you choose a paper streamer tail, make it approximately 30 inches long, although you may need to adjust the length to suit different wind conditions. If the kite tends to loop and spin in flight, lengthen the tail. If, on the other hand, the tail seems to restrict the kite's movement, shorten the tail. Since the function of a tail is to provide stability through both its weight and its air resistance, you can adjust the tail's effectiveness by fringing the paper or by adding a paper tassel at its end to create additional air resistance.

To make the true Chinese Fertility Kite, you should attach a rice sheaf to the juncture of each pair of spars on both sides of the kite. Tie or tape the sheaf at the base of the juncture so that the grains hang downward from the kite. If you are using a conventional kite tail, tie or tape a rice sheaf to the bottom of it in addition to the sheaves you attach to the spars.

The Chinese Fertility Kite   Scale: Grid Squares = 1"

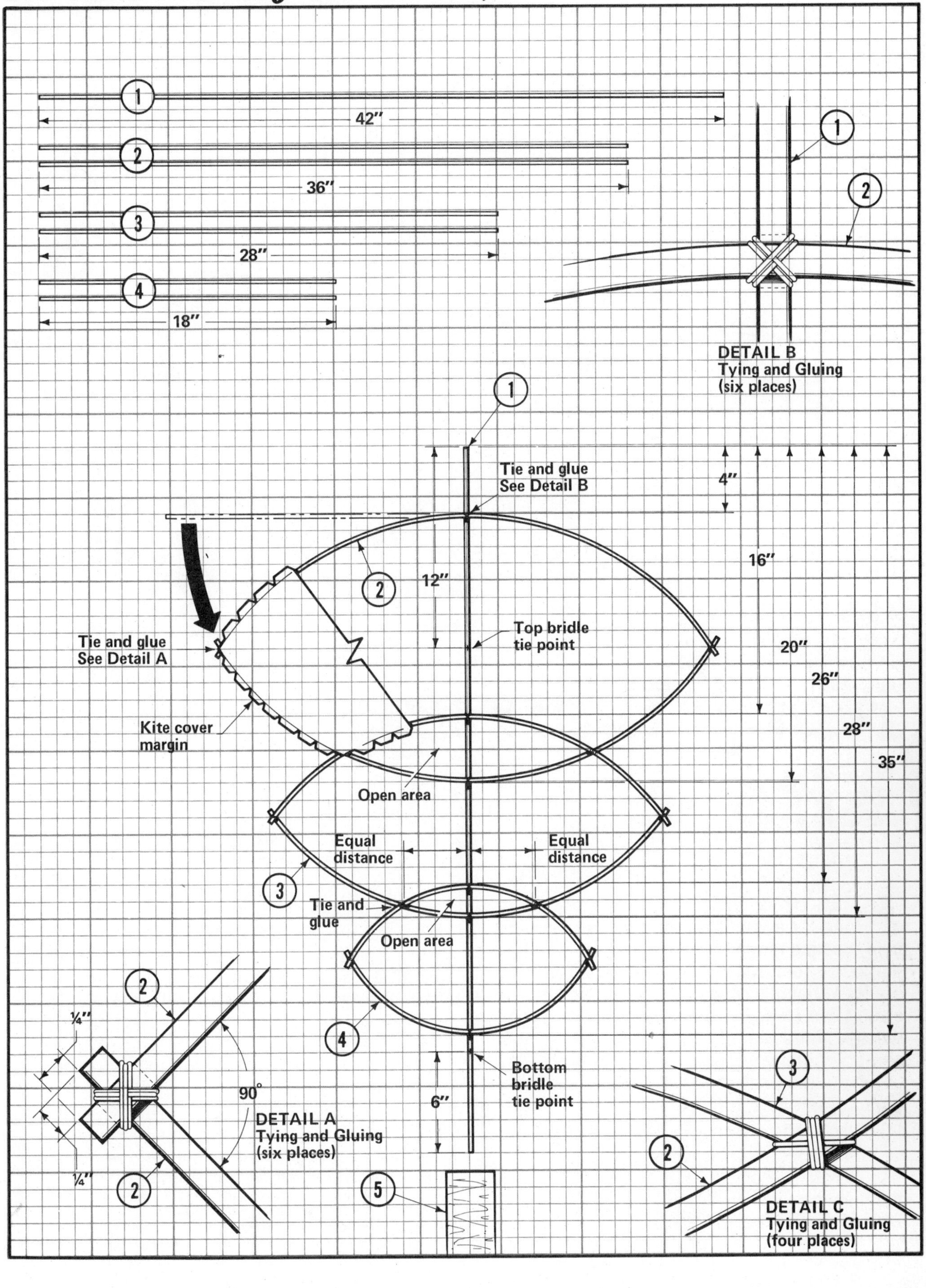

①

42"

②

36"

③

28"

④

18"

①

②

DETAIL B
Tying and Gluing
(six places)

①

Tie and glue
See Detail B

4"

②

12"

16"

Top bridle
tie point

20"

26"

Tie and glue
See Detail A

28"

35"

Kite cover
margin

Open area

Equal
distance

Equal
distance

③

Tie and
glue

Open area

②

¼"

④

90°

Bottom
bridle
tie point

③

¼"

②

6"

②

DETAIL A
Tying and Gluing
(six places)

⑤

DETAIL C
Tying and Gluing
(four places)

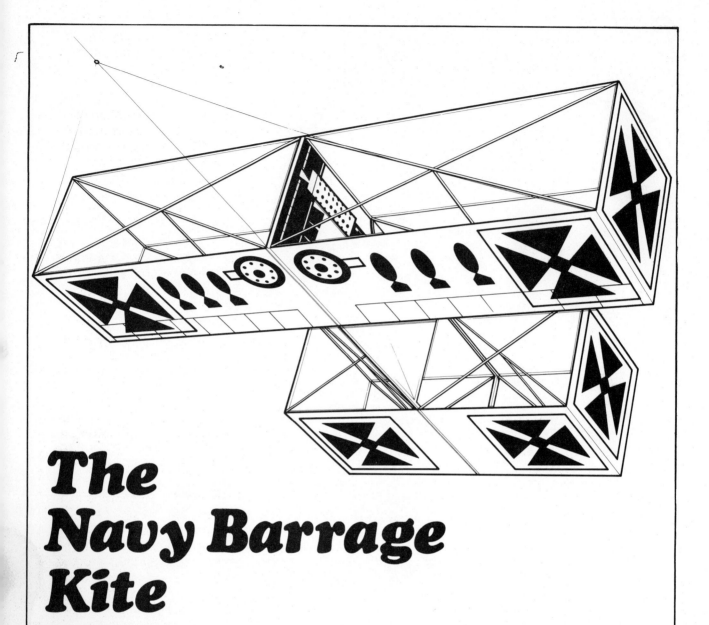

The Navy Barrage Kite

KITES HAVE BEEN used by many countries for a variety of military purposes: to hold practice targets, to carry men for scouting purposes, to transfer supplies, to hoist a camera for aerial photography, even to drop explosives. The United States, for example, used barrage kites during World War II to protect sea-going convoys from enemy aircraft. The box-type kites, tethered with wire, were flown approximately 2,000 feet above the ships. Each kite was about 20 feet wide, with additional wires hanging down in order to discourage enemy pilots from approaching. The wires could cut through the wings of the aircraft or damage propellers.

This unique kite is actually a scaled-down version of the true navy barrage kite. Resembling an airplane, the kite has a body section, two wing sections, and two tail sections. It will not, of course, be towed by a ship as were the true barrage kites, and despite the fact that it is much smaller than the towed versions, this kite still requires at least moderate to strong winds to stay aloft.

Editor's Note: The numbers and detail citations that appear in brackets [ ] throughout this chapter refer to the scale drawing of The Navy Barrage Kite.

Kite Frame Materials

THE FRAME OF the navy barrage kite should be constructed of slender wooden sticks of cypress, spruce, or pine, or of whitewood dowels. These woods are both strong and lightweight, and they can be obtained easily at most hobby, lumber, or hardware stores.

To construct the body section of the barrage kite, you will need two 36-inch spars [1] and three nine-inch spars [2]. For the kite's body section, obtain square-sectioned wood ⅜ of an inch thick; the wing sections and the tail sections require ¼-inch round dowels. To construct the wing sections, you will need ten spars [3] measuring 9¾ inches and eight spars [4] measuring 26½ inches. The tail section is composed of ten spars [5] 9¾ inches and eight spars [6] 16¾ inches.

How To Create A Navy Barrage Kite

CONSTRUCT THE body section of the kite first. Place the two 36-inch spars [1] horizontally on a flat surface so that they are parallel to each other and nine inches apart. Place one nine-inch spar [2] so that it runs perpendicular to the two 36-inch spars [1] at their right-hand ends. Nail and glue the shorter spar [2] to the two longer spars [1], drilling clearance holes and pilot holes to prevent cracking or splitting the spars [Detail A].

Now place one of the two remaining nine-inch spars [2] 24 inches from the first and fasten it to the two 36-inch spars [1] in the same manner. Then place the third nine-inch spar [2] vertically at the left side of the two 36-inch spars and fasten it to them as you have done twice previously.

The next step is to add two diagonal cords across this frame to reinforce it. First, cut two 27-inch pieces of string [7]; common four-ply cotton string is adequate for this purpose. Tie one end of the string [7] securely to the joint formed by the middle vertical spar [2] and the upper 36-inch spar [1]. Run the other end of the string to the corner diagonally across the 24-inch space, and lash it tightly to that frame joint. You must keep the string taut at all times. Tie the second string [7] so that it connects the opposite two corners of the frame and forms an "X" with the first string. Clip off any excess string at the points of lashing.

Apply glue to all the lashings, making certain that you soak the string and the knots thoroughly. Any glue that dries quickly and becomes tough rather than brittle is appropriate for this job. Now set the body section of the frame aside and allow it to dry completely.

You are now ready to form the two wing sections of the navy barrage kite. First, make a pencil mark at the exact center of each 26½-inch spar [4]. Next, drill a clearance hole at this point through both 26½-inch spars [4]. Then, use a small (one-inch) finishing nail to fasten two of the spars together at their exact centers to form an "X." Now drill a pilot hole in the end of the 9¾-inch spar [3], and, using the same nail, attach the center of the "X" to the end of this spar [3] [Detail B]. Make another "X" with two more 26½-inch spars [4] in the same manner that you did the first, and attach to the other end of the 9¾-inch spar [3].

Connect the four spars [4] of each "X" with four 9¾-inch spars [3] again using small nails. Now position the spars of the "X" frame so that the distance between the ends at the top and the ends at the bottom of the "X" is exactly nine inches.

When you are sure that the "X" is correctly positioned, lash the frame with string to hold it in place [Detail C]. Then cut "V" grooves in both ends of all the 9¾-inch corner wing spars [3] [Detail D].

Use either strong string or fishing line with 10-pound strength to create the guideline [8] that completes the wing frame. Lash the string [8] securely to the first "V" groove, and — keeping the string taut and maintaining the 9½-inch height dimension — continue it on to the next corner spar [3] of the "X;" tie it securely around the spar [3] at this joint. Continue guiding the string [8] on around the "X" frame, keeping it taut and knotting it around each corner spar until you have framed the entire "X" of the wing frame.

When you arrive back where you began, tie the two ends of the string together and clip off any excess. Repeat the same stringing process on the opposite side. When the wing frame is completely framed with string, soak each joint and knot of the guideline thoroughly with glue. Now set the wing section aside to dry, and construct the other wing section in exactly the same manner as you did the first.

With the body frame and two wing frames completed, you are ready to move on to the tail frames. You construct the two tail sections the same way that you assembled the wing sections. First, mark the centers of each 16¾-inch

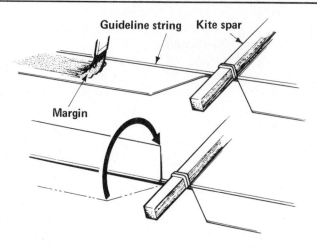

Guideline string   Kite spar

Margin

Apply glue to the margin and seal it over the frame, working slowly so as to avoid wrinkles and creases.

spar [6], and drill clearance holes in these spars as you previously did with the 26½-inch wing frame spars [4]. Next nail two spars [6] together at their center marks so that they form an "X" [Detail E]. Drill a pilot hole in the end of a 9¾-inch spar [5], and attach the "X" just as you did with the wing frame. Make another "X" in the same way and attach it to the other end of the 9¾-inch spar [5], forming a double "X." Position the spars of the "X" so that they are nine inches apart at the top and the bottom, and attach a string guideline [9] around the outside of the "X." Lash the string guideline to the "V" groove in each corner spar [5] in the same manner that you did for the wing sections, keeping the string taut at all times and maintaining the 9½-inch height dimension [Detail F]. When the framing is complete, be sure to soak the joints and knots with glue. Then construct a second tail section identical to the one you just made.

Preparing The Kite Cover

THE NEXT STEP in constructing the navy barrage kite is to prepare a covering. Lightweight cloth — e.g., heavy-gauge Mylar, Tyvek, ripstop nylon, etc. — is generally used to cover a barrage kite, although strong paper can be substituted.

First, measure the frame of one wing section to determine the size of the strip you will need to cover the top, one side, and the bottom of each wing section. Add a half-inch margin to all four sides of your measurement; you

will use the margin later to overlap and glue around the string and wood frame.

Now take sharp scissors and cut a panel [10] of covering for each wing section. Then cut another strip of covering 26 inches by 11 inches as a covering for the body frame of the kite. Finally, measure to determine the size of covering you will need to cover the top, one side, and the bottom of each tail section. Be sure to add a half-inch margin to each side of the measurement. When all five covering pieces are cut to size, notch them at the corners to allow for easy folding.

With the covering cut to size, it is time to decorate the kite cover. Refer to the chapter "Decorating The Kite" and to the full-color illustration for the Navy Barrage Kite.

You are now ready to attach the kite cover to the body frame and wings. First, place the flat body frame on the 26-inch by 11-inch section of covering [11]. Next, apply glue to the margin and seal it over the frame, working slowly to avoid making wrinkles or creases. Place the wing frame on the wing cover strip [10], and crease the half-inch margin on all sides. Then apply a neat line of glue to the four 9¾-inch spars [3] on what will be the covered end of the wing section. Carefully attach the covering [10] to the glued spars [3] being sure to keep the covering [10] smooth and straight. Working slowly and carefully, apply glue to the margin and seal it over the string guidelines [8] and the corner spars [3]. Cover the other wing section and tail sections in the same way.

Now join the sections of the barrage kite

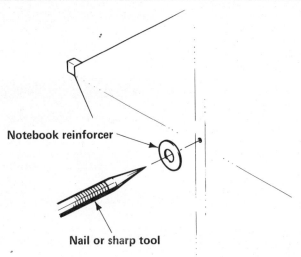

Notebook reinforcer

Nail or sharp tool

You must punch several holes in the kite cover in order to join together the various parts of The Navy Barrage Kite.

together [Details G and H]. Take a wing, and — using a nail or sharp-pointed tool — punch a hole in the cover directly over a 9¾-inch corner spar [5] one inch in from the trailing edge. The hole must be positioned so that when the cord [14] is pulled tight the corner spars [5] are pulled tight against the frame [1]. No tension must be put on the cover material [12]. Now punch another hole over the same spar one inch in from the leading edge, and follow the same procedure described above.

Next, make two more holes in the bottom of each wing section at the points directly below the first holes. If you have used paper for the kite cover material, apply glue or notebook reinforcers [13] around the holes to prevent tearing [Detail H]. When you have punched the holes in each wing section, repeat the process, making four similar holes in each of the tail sections.

Finally, make four holes in the covering of the body section. Holes must be punched and reinforced in the two positions at the top and the bottom that will line up with the holes in the wing sections.

Now cut eight-inch strips of strong cord [14] or fishing line. Place the wing sections in position on either side of the flat body with the holes aligned. Guide a piece of the cord [14] through the three holes at each position [Detail H], and lash the sections together securely. Tie the wing sections to the body frame at each of the other three points, and then tie the tail sections together, enclosing and securing the back of the body section in

the same manner.

The final step in constructing a navy barrage kite is to prepare a proper bridle [Detail J]. A three-legged bridle is necessary here to control the angle at which the surface of the kite meets the wind. The three points of attachment for the bridle legs are at the center and at each end of the wing sections along the bottom of the leading edge.

Punch a hole carefully (use a nail or sharp-pointed tool) in the bottom wing covering next to the joints formed by the bottom string guideline [8] and the wing spars [4]. Apply glue or a notebook reinforcer [13] around the hole to prevent tearing. Now cut a piece of cord [15] or fishing line to a length of 24 inches. Cut another length of cord [16] 72 inches long. Guide one end of the 24-inch cord through the hole in the middle of the wing and lash it securely to the frame of the kite. Tie the other end of this cord to a bridle ring — a curtain ring makes a good bridle ring. Now guide one end of the 72-inch cord [16] through the hole at one end of the wing and tie it tightly to the frame. Run the other end of the cord [16] through the bridle ring two or three times, and then guide this end through the hole at the other end of the wing and lash it securely to the frame. Slide the ring along the string until it is centered on the 72-inch length of cord [16].

You now have a full-fledged navy barrage kite, somewhat smaller than the ones used by the U.S. Navy, but one that will fly well and create an attention-gathering spectacle wherever you launch it.

The Navy Barrage Kite   Scale: Grid Squares = 1"

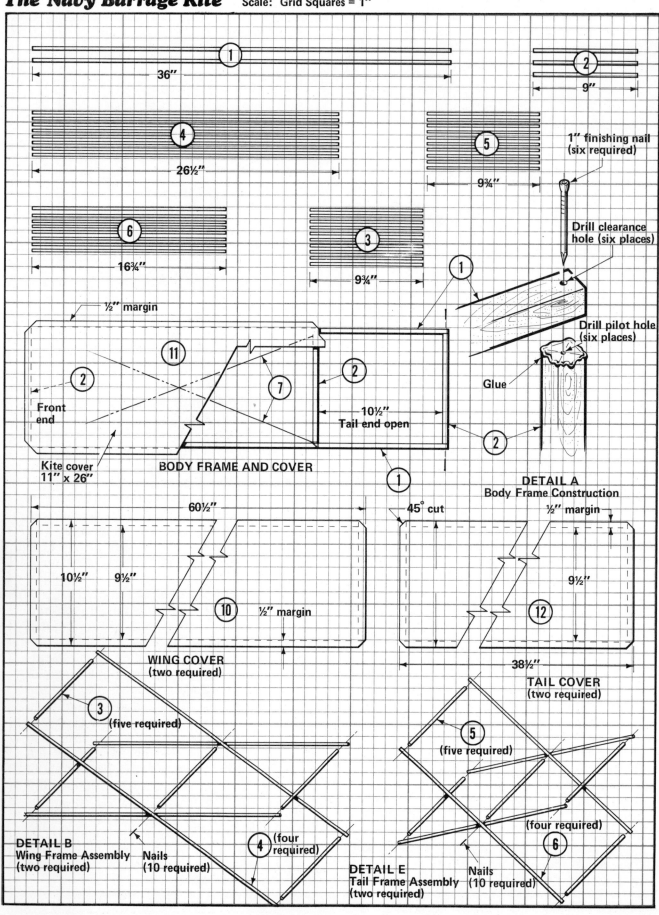

① 36"

② 9"

④ 26½"

⑤ 9¾"

⑥ 16¾"

③ 9¾"

1" finishing nail
(six required)

Drill clearance
hole (six places)

①

Drill pilot hole
(six places)

Glue

½" margin

⑪

②

⑦

②

Front
end

②

10½"
Tail end open

②

Kite cover
11" x 26"

BODY FRAME AND COVER

①

DETAIL A
Body Frame Construction

45° cut

½" margin

60½"

10½"   9½"

⑩   ½" margin

9½"

⑫

WING COVER
(two required)

38½"

TAIL COVER
(two required)

③

(five required)

⑤

(five required)

④ (four
required)

⑥

(four required)

DETAIL B
Wing Frame Assembly
(two required)   Nails
(10 required)

DETAIL E
Tail Frame Assembly
(two required)   Nails
(10 required)

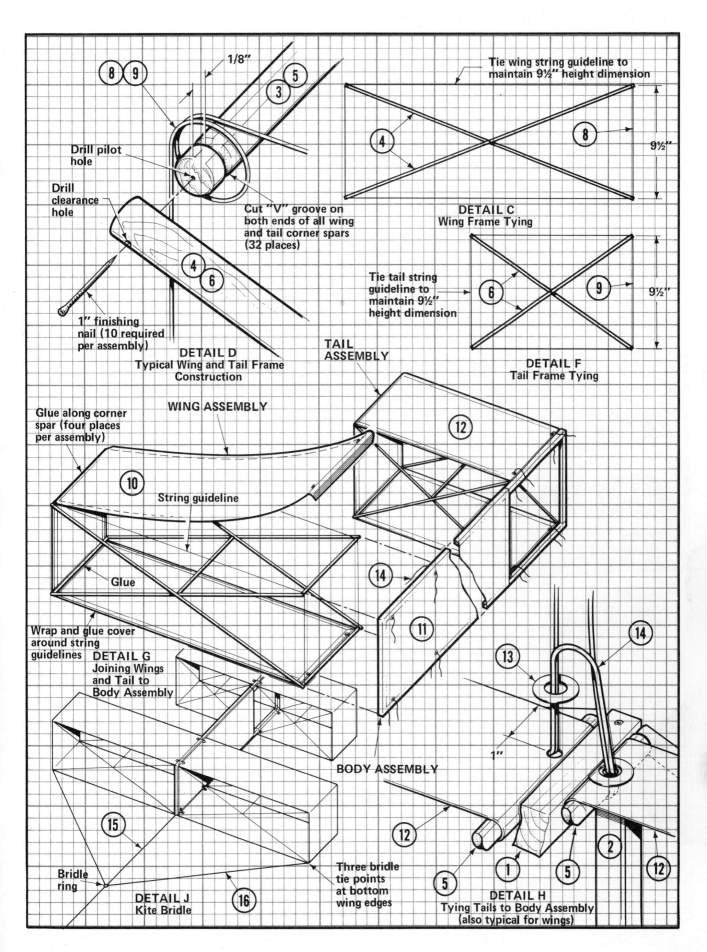

8 9

1/8"

3 5

Drill pilot
hole

Drill
clearance
hole

4 6

Cut "V" groove on
both ends of all wing
and tail corner spars
(32 places)

1" finishing
nail (10 required
per assembly)

DETAIL D
Typical Wing and Tail Frame
Construction

Tie wing string guideline to
maintain 9½" height dimension

4 8

9½"

DETAIL C
Wing Frame Tying

Tie tail string
guideline to
maintain 9½"
height dimension

6 9

9½"

DETAIL F
Tail Frame Tying

**TAIL
ASSEMBLY**

WING ASSEMBLY

Glue along corner
spar (four places
per assembly)

10

String guideline

12

14

11

Glue

Wrap and glue cover
around string
guidelines

DETAIL G
Joining Wings
and Tail to
Body Assembly

BODY ASSEMBLY

13 14

1"

15

12

Bridle
ring

DETAIL J
Kite Bridle

16

Three bridle
tie points
at bottom
wing edges

5 1 5 2 12

DETAIL H
Tying Tails to Body Assembly
(also typical for wings)

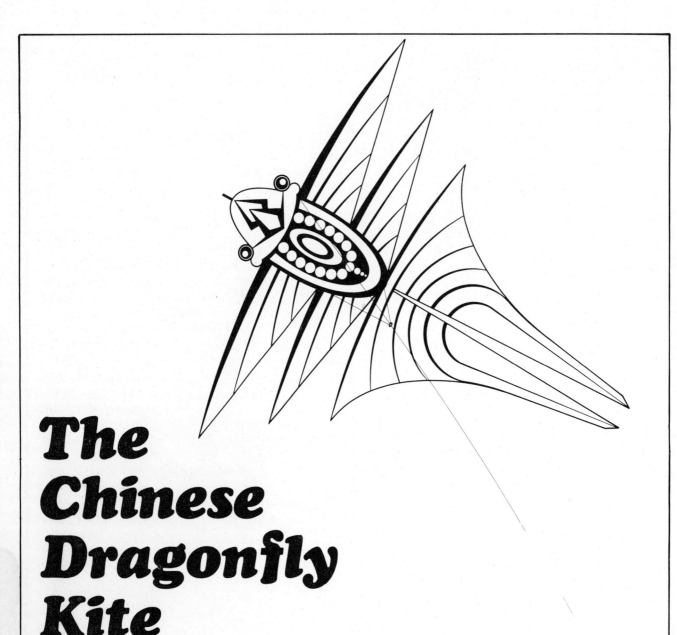

The Chinese Dragonfly Kite

KITES FASHIONED after insects are among the most intricate and colorful that one sees in the sky. The diversity of shapes and construction is virtually endless, which is why the insect kite is so popular with creative kite makers and why it is so often an entry in kite contests.

The giant dragonfly kite described here is an adaptation of the Chinese design. It is a very intricate kite to construct, and the body must be formed carefully to maintain symmetry. With its spinning eyes and fluttering wings, however, it offers a most unusual and dramatic spectacle as it rides the wind in flight.

Kite Frame Materials

SPLIT BAMBOO is the ideal material for the frame of the dragonfly kite. It is strong and lightweight, and, most importantly, it retains its shape after being bent. You can purchase split bamboo at most craft stores and hobby shops, but you may find exactly what you need in dis-

Editor's Note: The numbers and detail citations that appear in brackets [ ] throughout this chapter refer to the scale drawing of The Chinese Dragonfly Kite.

carded outdoor porch shades. You can, of course, split your own bamboo from an old bamboo cane or pole. Just make sure that you wind up with bamboo spars that are no larger than a quarter-inch square.

How To Create A Chinese Dragonfly Kite

TO CONSTRUCT the frame of this kite, you will need one 72-inch spar [1] for the body of the dragonfly, one 32-inch spar [2] for the centerpole, and two 17-inch spars [3] for the cross-supports. The wings of the dragonfly kite require one 57-inch spar [4], one 55-inch spar [5], and one 46-inch spar [6]. In addition, two 8-inch strips of bamboo [7] are needed to form the eyes and two 6-inch strips [8] to shape the head.

Cut the spars to size, and then test the three wing spars [4, 5, and 6], the centerpole [2], and the two cross-support spars [3] for balance. You do this by drawing a pencil line at the exact center of each spar and then balancing the spar at its center on the edge of a knife blade. If one side tends to go down, the spar is not balanced, and you must correct the imbalance by paring or sandpapering the heavier side until the spar balances properly. Balance is an essential requirement for successful kite-making.

When you are satisfied that the spars are balanced, you are ready to join the centerpole [2] and cross-spar supports [3]. Place the centerpole [2] on a flat surface, and position the cross-spar supports [3] in an "X" over the centerpole [2]. The point of intersection of the "X" should be 16 inches from the top of the centerpole [2] at the exact center mark of the two cross-spar supports [3].

Now lash the point of juncture with strong, non-stretching, and non-bulky string; common four-ply cotton string is adequate. Lash the two cross-spar supports [3] and the centerpole [2] in position by taking at least two turns through each diagonal of the crossing point. Then weave the string over and under the spars, and tie it with a square knot. Cut off any extra string that remains after knotting.

The remaining spars — those other than the centerpole [2] and cross-support spars [3] — must undergo certain preparations before they can be formed into their appropriate shapes. First check each of these spars to be sure that they bend evenly along their full length and that they are relatively free of irregularities like bumps or ridges which would adversely affect their balance. These spars must be bent into shape, and the easiest way to prepare the spars for bending is simply to soak them in water for several hours. After soaking, they should bend easily without splitting or cracking.

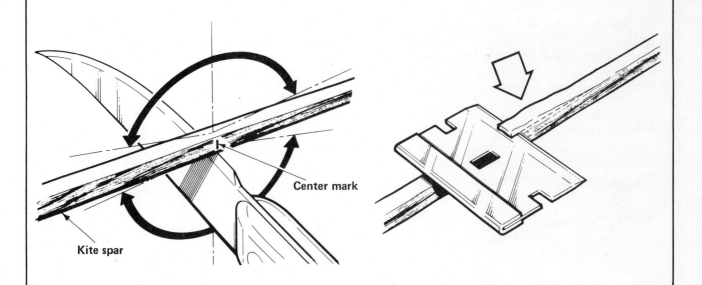

Center mark

Kite spar

(LEFT) Place the spar at its center point on the edge of a knife blade to test for balance. (RIGHT) Trim the spar as necessary until it balances.

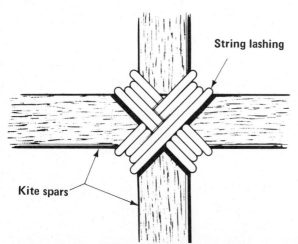

String lashing

Kite spars

Lash the cross-spar supports to the centerpole by wrapping the point of juncture with string.

When the spars become flexible, you are ready to form the frame of the dragonfly's body. Take the long 72-inch spar [1] and notch it at each end. Now apply glue to the notched ends and overlap them, forming an oval shape. Make sure that the glue you use is one that dries quickly and that does not become brittle. Then lash this joint with string [Detail C]. When tying two surfaces that run parallel, like the point of juncture here, it is best to make two lashings as far apart as possible. Secure each of these two lashings with a square knot or tie a regular knot twice. Then soak the double lashing and the entire area of overlap thoroughly with glue, and allow it to dry before proceeding further.

The next step is to place the oval body frame [1] over the centerpole [2] and cross-spar support frame [3], with the overlap area of the oval at the top of the centerpole [2]. Lash the oval body frame [1] to the centerpole

[2] at the top of the centerpole [2]; make sure that you take the string through both diagonals of the juncture. Then lash the oval body frame [1] to the centerpole [2] at the bottom of the frame; make certain that the point of juncture is formed at the center mark of the oval body frame.

Now shape the oval body frame [1] so that it will be slightly larger in the center than at the two ends, bulging to a width of approximately 12 inches in the portion between the ends of the cross-support spars [3]. Remember to maintain absolute symmetry. When you are satisfied that the spars are properly positioned, lash the oval body frame [1] to the cross-support spars [3] at the four points where they intersect.

The next step involves attaching the wings spars [4, 5, and 6] to the centerpole [2] and to the oval body frame [1]. First, place the 57-inch spar [4] across the centerpole [2] at a 90-degree angle; the point of juncture must be 11 inches down from the top of the centerpole [2]. Make sure that the center of the wing spar [4] is directly over the centerpole [2], and then lash the centerpole [2] and the wing spar [4] together securely. Next, lash each side of the oval body frame [1] to the wing spar [4]; the points of juncture must be six inches out from the center of the wing spar [4]. Finally, lash the wing spar [4] to the cross-support spars [3] at the two points of intersection.

Now place the 55-inch wing spar [5] across the centerpole [2] at a 90-degree angle; this point of juncture must be 21 inches down from the top of the centerpole [2]. Lash this wing spar [5] to the oval body frame [1] at a point six inches out from the center of the wing spar [5]. Then lash the wing spar [5] to the cross-support spars [3].

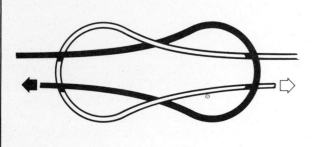

After lashing, tie the string ends into a square knot.

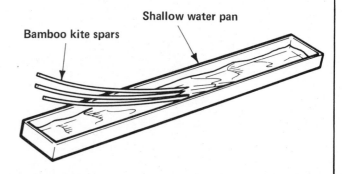

Shallow water pan

Bamboo kite spars

Soak the spars in water to prepare them for bending.

Place the 46-inch wing spar [6] across the centerpole [2] at a point 30 inches down from the top of the centerpole [2]. Attach the wing spar [6] to the centerpole [2] at the wing spar's [6] center point, and then lash the wing spar [6] to the oval body frame [1] at the points where the two intersect.

The final step in forming the wing frame for the dragonfly kite involves bowing each wing spar three inches. First, cut V grooves at both ends of each wing spar [4, 5 and 6] [Detail B]. Then cut two pieces of string to a length of 30 inches, and attach the end of one strand of string to the right-hand end of the 57-inch wing spar [4]. Lash the other end of this string to the oval body frame [1] at the intersection of the 55-inch wing spar [5] and the cross-support spar [3]. Repeat the same process to form the wing on the other side of the kite.

Now, using two 33-inch lengths of string, bow the 55-inch wing spar [5] by lashing the strings to the oval body frame [1] at the intersection of the 46-inch wing spar [6] and the oval body frame [1]. Finally, bow the 46-inch wing spar [6] with two 29-inch lengths of string, attaching the strings to the ends of the wing spar [6] and to the oval body frame [1] at the intersection of the centerpole [2] and the oval body frame [1] at the bottom of the kite.

To complete the total frame of the dragonfly kite, you must now shape the head and attach the eyes. First, notch the six-inch strips of bamboo [2] at both ends and overlap the notched ends to form a circle. Next, glue at the point of overlap, and lash this joint with string [Detail C]. Then lash the bamboo circle [8] to the oval body frame on both sides of the head [Detail A]. Next, form two circles in the same manner with the 8-inch strips [7] to create the eye frames. Place the eye frames [7] in position, and then tie them securely to the oval body frame [1] at the point of juncture [Detail A]. Finally, tie the eye frames [7] to the head bulge [8] at the point they abut.

At this point, you must test the balance of the entire frame. Place one end of the centerpole [2] on a table and rest the other end on the tip of your finger. The frame should rest along a horizontal plane. If it tends to dip to one side, the frame is not balanced and you must correct the problem. First, check to see if the cross-support spars [3] and wing spars [4, 5 and 6] are centered exactly over the centerpole [2]. If they are not, adjust the lashings. If the frame still fails to balance, the problem is prob-

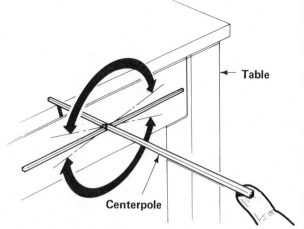

Test the kite frame for balance; it should rest on a horizontal plane.

ably unequal weight in the spars on either side of the centerpole [2]. Whittle or pare the heavier side down until proper balance is achieved.

When the frame balances apply a thorough soaking of glue to the string of all the lashings; then set the frame aside to dry.

Preparing The Kite Cover

USE A LIGHTWEIGHT paper for the covering of the dragonfly kite. Anything from wrapping paper to tissue paper, shelf paper, crepe paper, or imitation Japanese paper (found in most art supply stores) is suitable.

Place the kite frame on the cover material, and then use a pencil to trace around the outside edge of the frame — except for all the eyes — allowing a half-inch margin all around the frame. Later, you will glue this margin to enclose and seal the frame. Extend the tracing on the kite cover to include the descending, tapered pair of wings which will serve as a double tail for stabilization. The two descending wings should be 40 inches each.

When you finish tracing the pattern, cut out the kite cover with sharp scissors to insure a clean, even edge. Notch the edges of the margin to enable smooth folding.

Now, with the covering cut to size, it is time to decorate. Refer to the chapter "Decorating The Kite" and to the full-color illustration of the Chinese Dragonfly Kite for ideas.

When the kite cover is decorated, attach it to the frame. Crease the margin over the frame, enclosing the frame completely except at the

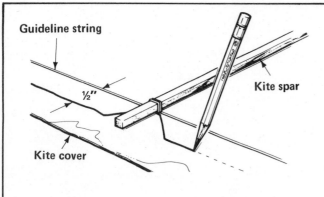

Guideline string

½"

Kite spar

Kite cover

Trace around the outside edge of the frame, leaving a half-inch margin.

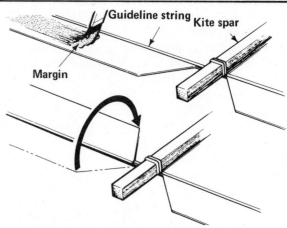

Guideline string

Kite spar

Margin

Apply glue to the margin and seal it over the edge of the frame.

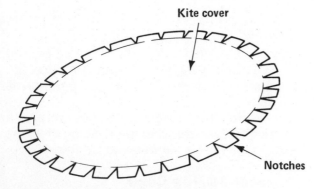

Kite cover

Notches

Notch the margin to assure smooth folding.

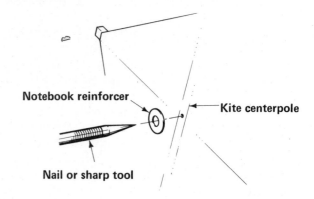

Notebook reinforcer

Kite centerpole

Nail or sharp tool

Punch holes in the kite cover for the bridle string.

bottom of the lower pair of wings. Next, apply glue to the margin and seal it over the frame. Try to avoid wrinkles and creases which by their bulk and unevenness might hinder flight.

To make the two spinning eyes [9], cut two circles from strong, heavy-duty paper of any color you wish. The diameter of each circle should be approximately 1¾ inches. Then punch two small holes through each paper circle [9] and insert a toothpick through each. Glue the ends of the toothpicks to the bamboo eye frames [7] so that the eyes [9] are free to spin when the kite is in flight.

The final step is to prepare a three-legged bridle which will control the angle at which the surface of the dragonfly kite meets the wind. With a nail or other pointed object, carefully punch a hole in the kite cover on both sides over the point where the oval body frame [1] is lashed to the top of the head bulge. Make a third hole above the intersection of the centerpole [2] and the bottom wing spar [6]. Apply a notebook reinforcer around the three holes.

Now cut a piece of string to a length of 60 inches. Guide one end of the string through the hole at the upper left of the kite, and lash it securely to the oval body frame [1]. Guide the other end of the string through a bridle ring — a curtain ring makes an ideal bridle ring — two or three times. Position the bridle ring so that it is approximately at the center of the length of the string. Then guide the free end of the string through the hole at the upper right of the kite, and lash it securely to the oval body frame [1]. Cut another piece of string 25 inches long, and attach one end of this string to the bridle ring; run the other end through the reinforced hole near the bottom of the kite, and then tie it to the centerpole [2]. Do not trim the excess string because you may need it to make bridle adjustments to accommodate various wind conditions.

You have now completed one of the most unique and dazzling of all the kites you can create. The dragonfly kite will fly well in light to gentle winds.

The Dragonfly Kite

Scale: Grid Squares = 1"

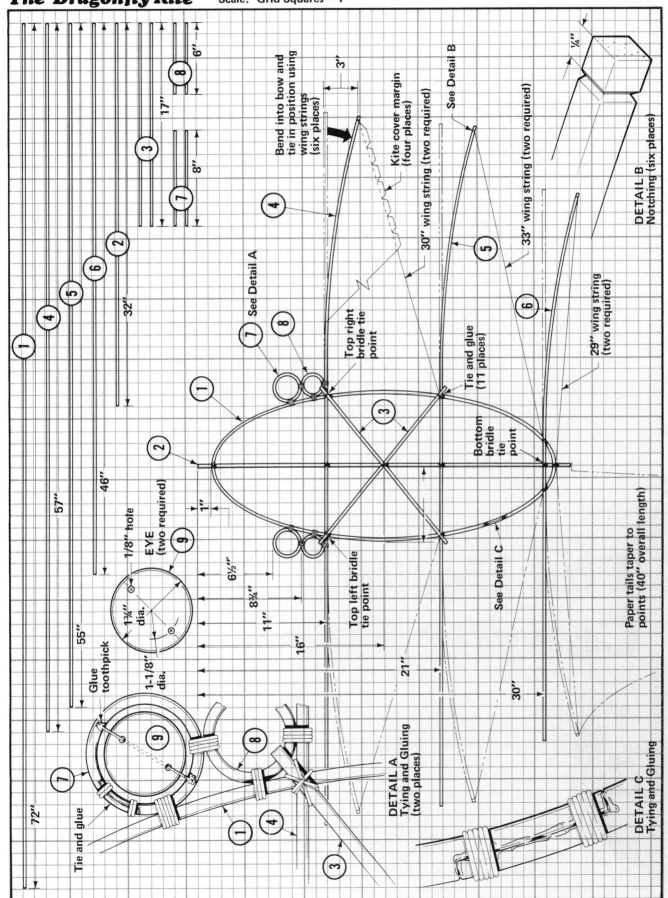

6"

⑧

17"

③

8"

⑦

③

32"

②

⑥

⑤

④

46"

①

57"

55"

72"

Tie and glue

Glue toothpick

1/8" hole

EYE
(two required)

⑨

1-3/4" dia.

1-1/8" dia.

1"

6½"

8¾"

11"

16"

21"

30"

⑨

⑦

⑧

①

④

③

Bend into bow and tie in position using wing strings (six places)

3"

Kite cover margin (four places)

See Detail B

④

See Detail A

⑦

⑧

①

②

③

⑤

⑥

Top right bridle tie point

Top left bridle tie point

30" wing string (two required)

33" wing string (two required)

29" wing string (two required)

Tie and glue (11 places)

Bottom bridle tie point

See Detail C

Paper tails taper to points (40" overall length)

DETAIL A
Tying and Gluing (two places)

DETAIL B
Notching (six places)

¼"

DETAIL C
Tying and Gluing

123

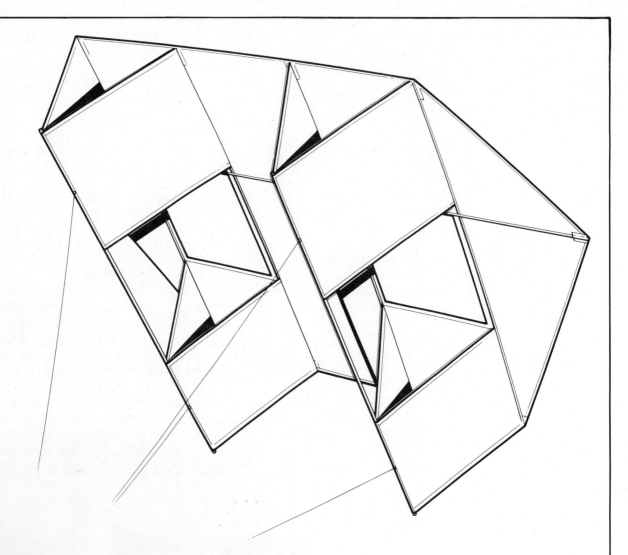

The Double Conyne Kite

THE CONYNE KITE, as it has come to be called, is essentially a triangular box kite with wings. It incorporates the lifting advantages of a flat kite with the stability of a box kite. Invented by Silas Conyne in 1902, the design was adapted and used by the French army; as a result, the kite is also commonly called the French Military Kite. The kite described here, the elaborate Double Conyne Kite, is a variation of the basic Conyne kite, and it creates a grand spectacle in flight.

How To Create A Double Conyne Kite

TO CONSTRUCT the frame of the Double Conyne Kite, you will need four upright spars and two central spars [1], all cut to a length of

> **Editor's Note:** The numbers and detail citations that appear in brackets [ ] throughout this chapter refer to the scale drawing of The Double Conyne Kite.

38 inches. In addition, you will need one 56-inch spar [2] that will serve as the cross-wing spreader. Wooden sticks of cypress, spruce or pine or even quarter-inch whitewood dowels can be used for the spars and cross-wing spreader. These woods are lightweight but strong, and you can find them at most hobby shops, lumber markets or hardware stores.

After you cut the seven spars to their proper length, you must test each one for balance. Balance is an extremely important requirement for successful kite-making. Test the spars by placing a pencil mark at the exact center of each spar's length, and then balance the spar on the edge of a knife blade at that point. If the spar does not hover on a horizontal plane, it is not balanced, and you must correct the situation by paring or sandpapering the heavier side until balance is achieved.

When you are satisfied that the spars are balanced, put them aside for the moment.

Preparing The Kite Cover

THE DOUBLE Conyne Kite is generally covered with lightweight cloth — heavy-gauge Mylar, Tyvek, ripstop nylon, or even very strong paper can be used. After you select your cover material, you can proceed with the task of decorating it. Refer to the chapter "Decorating the Kite" and to the full-color illustration of the Double Conyne Kite for ideas.

Cut a rectangular piece of the covering [3] to the following dimensions: 38 inches long by 55 inches wide. Then mark this panel of cover material at 11-inch intervals. Measure from the left and draw a straight pencil line from top to bottom at each interval. Now, using a ruler or straightedge, draw a diagonal line from the top of the first 11-inch line to a point on the left edge of the covering 13 inches down from the top. Then draw another diagonal line from this point to the bottom of the first 11-inch interval line. Fold the cover material in half and cut along these two slanted lines to create a symmetrical, five-sided cover shape.

At this point, carefully fold and then stitch a one-quarter-inch hem around the outside of the entire cover panel. Cut notches in the margin at the corners to allow for easy folding.

You must now mark the position of the kite's two openings, or vents. Draw a horizontal line between the first and second 11-inch interval lines, again at a point 13 inches down from the top. Draw another horizontal line 25 inches from the top, creating a vertical, rectangular box. Now adjust the vertical sides of this box by drawing new vertical lines that are half an inch within the interval lines; the result is a box that is now 12 inches long by 10 in-

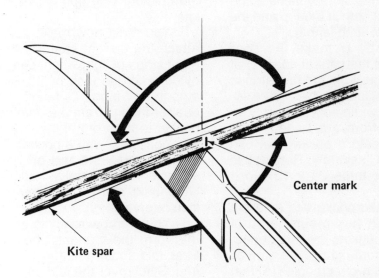

Center mark

Kite spar

Test a spar for balance by marking its center point and then placing the point on the edge of a knife blade.

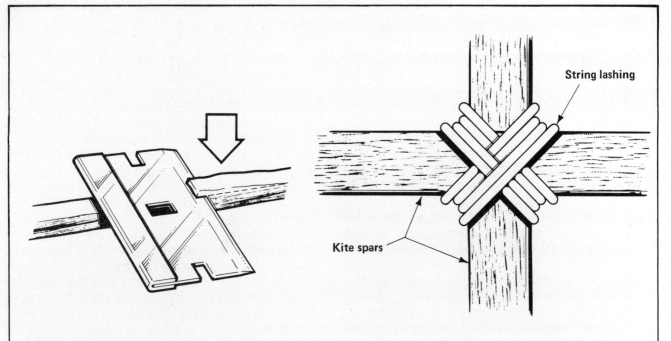

String lashing

Kite spars

(LEFT) Correct a spar imbalance by paring down the heavier side. (RIGHT) Lash the spars together by wrapping a strong lightweight string at least twice through both diagonals at the point of juncture.

ches wide. Mark the other vent in between the third and fourth interval lines in exactly the same manner, and then cut out both vents. Cut notches at the corners of each vent so that you can crease and stitch a quarter-inch hem around the edge of each vent.

The next step involves cutting the strips [4] for the two sides of the triangular boxes. Cut four strips 24½ inches by 12½ inches, and then sew a quarter-inch hem in the top and the bottom along each 24½-inch length.

You are now ready to make the spar pockets which will hold the central spar [1] at the front of each triangle. Fold the first strip in half lengthwise, and stitch the two sides together along the entire width approximately an eighth of an inch in from the folded edge [Detail A]. This will create a pocket that can hold the central spar [1] securely. Repeat this process with the other three 24 x 12½-inch strips.

You must now make pockets to hold the cross-wing spreader [2] at the outside tip of each wing [3]. These pockets are most effective if they are made from lightweight canvas or reinforced nylon. Cut two rectangles [5] that measure two inches by one inch. Trim one end of each rectangle [5] so that it comes to a point and matches the shape of the outside wing tip

[3]. Now cut two squares [6] that measure one inch by one inch. Cut one end of each square so that both come to points matching the points of the rectangles [5]; curve the other end of each square to allow for insertion of the cross-wing spreader [2]. Now, place each of the squares [6] over its matching rectangle [5], and then sew them together in position on the outside wing tips on the back side of the kite.

You must now make spar pockets [7] to attach the upright spars to the kite face. Cut eight strips of lightweight canvas or reinforced nylon, each an inch by 13 inches. Fold each strip in half along its length and stitching it a quarter-inch in from the unfolded edge. Sew a pocket to the front of the cover at each of the four positions, with a pocket [7] on both sides above each vent and on both sides below each vent. The unfolded edge of each pocket [7] should rest on the lines marking the 11-inch intervals.

You are now ready to attach the strips [4] that form the triangular box of the kite face. First, fold under a half-inch of material at each end. Stitch over the fold, sewing the triangular strip to the main cover [3]. Now insert the two central spars [1] in the two pockets at the front of the triangular box [4] and insert the four

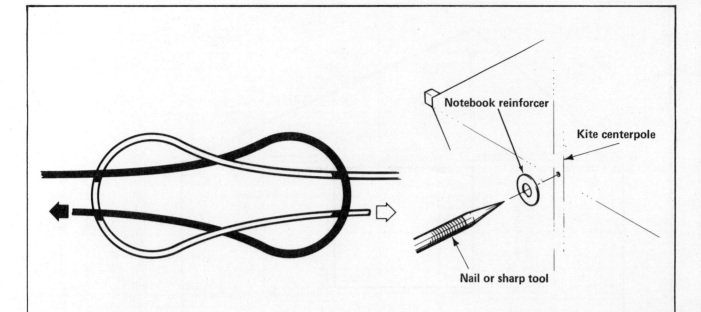

(LEFT) After weaving the string over and under the spars, tie the ends in a square knot. (RIGHT) Before you can attach the bridle, punch holes in the kite cover and apply notebook reinforcers to prevent tearing.

upright spars [1] in the pockets [7] on the kite's cover. Sew all pockets closed at the top and bottom of the kite. Next, insert the long cross-wing spreader [2] in the appropriate pockets [5 and 6] on the back of the kite.

Lash the upright spars [1] to the cross-wing spreader [2] at the four points where they intersect. Lash the spars together with strong lightweight string (four-ply cotton string serves the purpose) by taking at least two turns through both diagonals of the point of juncture. Then weave the string over and under the spars before tying it with a square knot. Clip off any excess string.

Apply glue to the lashings, soaking the string of the joints and knots thoroughly. Any quick-drying glue that becomes tough rather than brittle is appropriate for this job. When you finish gluing, set the kite aside and allow it to dry.

The final step in building the Double Conyne Kite is to prepare a proper bridle. This kite requires a compound bridle, one that you attach to the central spars [1] at the point of each triangle. The success of the kite in flight is in part dependent on these triangular boxes [4] staying open, and the bridle attachment at these four points is designed to keep the boxes [4] open.

With a nail or sharp-pointed tool, carefully punch a hole 6¼ inches from the top of each triangular box [4] and directly over the central spar [1]. Apply glue or a notebook reinforcer to the hole to prevent tearing. Now cut two 96-inch pieces of string or fishing line, guide one end of one string through the hole of one of the upper triangles [4], and lash it securely to the central spar [1]. Tie an overhand loop in the string at a point 40 inches from the point of attachment. Then guide the other end of the string through the hole in the triangle [4] directly below the hole to which you just attached the first end of the string. Lash it securely to the central spar [1] as well. Now tie the other string to the other two bridle points in the same manner, making sure to position the overhand loop in the same position as you did on the first string.

Cut another piece of string 96 inches long and tie one end to one of the overhand loops. Wrap the other end through a bridle ring (a curtain ring serves the purpose well) two or three times, and then tie this string securely to the other overhand loop. Position the bridle ring halfway between the two overhand loops.

You now have created a handsome kite design fashioned after the unique invention of Silas Conyne.

The Double Conyne Kite

Scale: Grid Squares = 1"

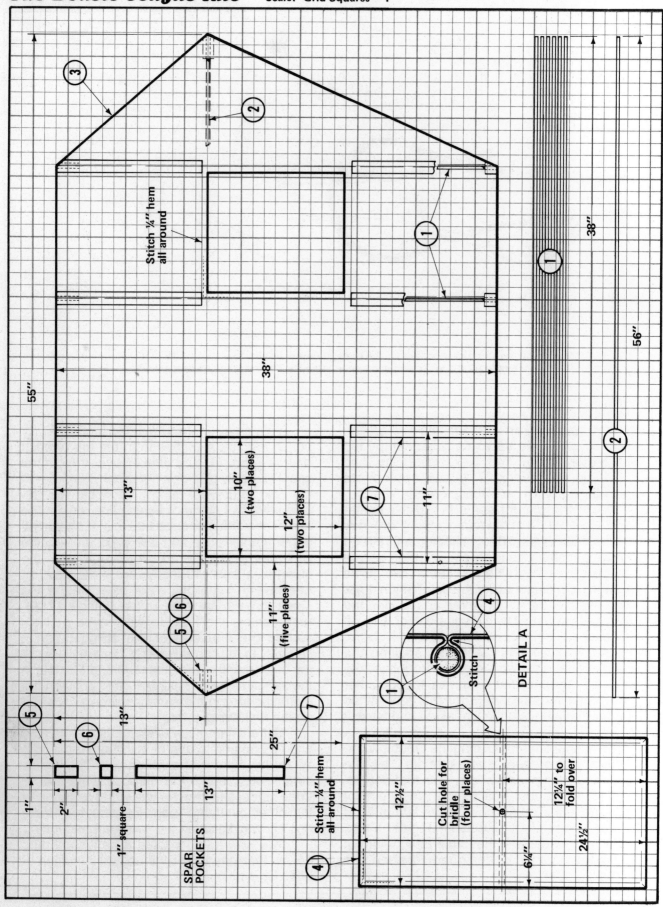

Stitch ¼" hem all around

55"

38"

56"

38"

13"

10" (two places)

12" (two places)

11"

11" (five places)

DETAIL A

Stitch

Cut hole for bridle (four places)

12½"

6¼"

12¼" to fold over

24½"

Stitch ¼" hem all around

25"

13"

1" square

2"

1"

13"

SPAR POCKETS